The Blood Covenant Bride -

Prophetic Writings by Gavin Finley MD

Edited by J. Scott Husted

Copyright Release

These articles by Gavin Finley are offered into the Kingdom of God for the purpose of fulfilling the **Great Commission** of our Lord Jesus Christ, to "make disciples of all nations". None of the articles are copyrighted. They are offered freely to all. You may abbreviate them, make abstracts of them, and expand on them as you wish for use in Christian ministry. The articles, in whole or in part, may be linked, copied, or printed out for distribution into any and all venues, media, and publishing outlets without any restriction whatsoever. The time is late. I **WANT** this information to go viral. With these articles go my prayers and best wishes to all. –Gavin Finley

Find more at *endtimepilgrim.org*

This edition Copyright 2014 by J. Scott Husted

ISBN 978-1-312-33805-0

Contents

Blood Covenant Christianity   5

The Flight to Mystery Bozrah   79

The Bozrah Exile   115

The Bozrah Deliverance   145

Blood Covenant Christianity
The Witness of the New Covenant

The New Covenant Is A Blood Covenant.
And The True Church Is The Bride Of Christ.
The Bride Actively Participates In The Covenant.
Holy History Will Most Certainly Call For Her Witness.
She Signs And Seals The New Covenant With Her Bridegroom.
Her Witness Is Required Before The New Covenant Can Be Executed.
It Is Necessary Before The Marriage Of The Lamb Can Be Consummated.
The 5th Seal Witness Of The Saints Will Be Seen Before Men And Angels.
Then Comes The 6th Seal And The Awesome Deliverance At The Last Day.

A devotional/exhortational essay
by Gavin Finley MD
Email: gwfinley@cox.net

HAS JESUS 'DONE IT ALL'?

As Christians of the western world we are generally contented in our faith.
Many of us have become satisfied with what we have been told.
And the gist of that message we receive and live by is very often this.
"Jesus has **done it all**".

This statement is somewhat ambiguous. And what often follows is this.
"He did it all". ----> "Therefore there is no call on me to do anything in response."

Yes, it is true that the blood of Christ has been shed. Here we see the purchase price for our salvation. It is the holy blood of the spotless sinless Sacrifice Lamb of God. The atoning blood of Jesus/Yeshua is the complete and finished sacrifice. It can have nothing added from us. The blood of atonement is the bridal price, the purchase price for our redemption. The 'bridal price' for our redemption has been fully paid by the Bridegroom. Jesus Christ in His death, burial, and resurrection has totally and completely reconciled the account between God and His covenant people. Jesus/Yeshua has totally paid the penalty for sin. That penalty was His death on the cross. So this first matter of the covenant, paying the purchase price of our redemption, is finished. Our great salvation has been fully paid for.

The issue of the price of our redemption is a very important legal and accounting matter. And yes, the heavenly account for the purchase of our salvation has been settled. The debt for our sin has been canceled. The Bridegroom, our Lord Jesus, has picked up the tab. And the bridal price has been paid in full. With His shed blood our Messiah has made total provision for His Bride, the Congregation of Israel, or as we term it, "the Church". This is the great salvation which the Gospel brings. This is the message of redemption and salvation we have heard. This is the Gospel, the Light of Israel that shines out by God's grace to the Jewish House of Israel first, to the lost ten tribes of Israel, and to their companions being drawn out of the Gentiles, (or heathen nations), as an ekklesia/congregation/church. It is all one in Christ our Messiah, a single Elect company, drawn from every nation, race, and tribe. This is the Good News of the Gospel. All across this world, this wonderful message is bringing redemption to all who will hear. And this is the great salvation promised to all who respond in faith believing.

IS OUR FAITH A UNILATERAL CONTRACT TO ACQUIRE A "FREE TICKET TO HEAVEN"? OR IS IT A TWO-WAY BLOOD COVENANT BETWEEN US AND OUR MESSIAH, A COMMITMENT UNTO DEATH? HAS OUR SALVATION OF "CHEAP GRACE" BECOME JUST ANOTHER EXAMPLE OF A CHURCH MARKETED "INDULGENCE"? OR IS IT A BLOOD COVENANT IN WHICH WE WILL SELL OUT ALL WE HAVE AND ALL WE ARE FOR OUR SAVIOR AND LORD?

This is sad to have to report. Nevertheless it is true in all too many cases. Our western merchant churches have been driven by the desire to profit. Church ministries are in a "price war" with ministerial competitors. And so the game for today's religi-business is all too clear. It is to "sell" the Gospel to the masses and for the cheapest possible price. Such are the ways of Mammon. In a profit driven economy the game is to "capture the religious market" targeting the Churchgoing Christians who are average or "middle of the pack" in their devotion.

The results of all this is all too apparent. The message of the Gospel has been brought down low. The bid to make Christianity seeker friendly has resulted in a lukewarm message that causes it to be scarcely recognizable as the faith that was once delivered to the saints. Christians of former times would be hard pressed to identify it as the true Christian faith. The message we are presenting now is in many cases not the Gospel at all. It is a figment of our own self-seeking imaginations. A free ticket to heaven just fell out of the sky. And we grabbed it. We do not stop to think or to meditate on what this means.

This is an awful state of affairs. We are rich and popular and in need of nothing. We are jam packed full of religion. And yet we do not know the God who comes inside us to bring us His righteousness and His grace. Our enemies are all around us putting their spin on the Bible. And we do not know it. We continue to be drawn ever deeper into compromise with the powers of this world. All too often we are inclined to dodge the higher calling of our faith. We are like the proverbial frog in the heated water bath our spiritual condition is becoming more and more tenuous. We are about to be cooked! And yet here in the western church we are quite unaware of the perilous situation we are now in.

What has happened to us? We started out with the true faith that was once delivered to the saints. But then we were enticed and seduced by Mammon. We proceeded to re-process, re-engineer, and re-package the message. The Gospel is now a "product" for sale to the masses. In order to sell it the message is processed and refined so as not to offend anyone. Then it is artificially sweetened to render it palatable and appealing for the average middle of the road carnal Christian. This is the **profitable** way to handle religion to make for "success".

Churchmen are in a bind here. In many cases they are hired by the state or by denominational boards.
Even pastors in the free churches are hired and fired by their deacon boards.
In many cases deacons are made up of businessmen, beholden to the "bottom line".
(Or so they think).

But they are wrong.
There is a true "bottom line" beneath the dollars written on the ledger.
And it is written in blood.

So Christian ministers are financially shackled. Sad to say, they are beholden to market forces. Church offerings, pastoral income, pastoral popularity, and mortgage payments on elaborate church buildings; are all factors that come into the equation here. And so churchmen must "sell" their religious sermons as wares. The customers in the pews, and "customer satisfaction" are the key here.

Pastors are oftentimes beholden to fickle but financially influential church members. These are religious consumers who by reason of past finacial contributions to the church think they own the church and "hire" the pastor to serve them. So the concern about ministers of God becoming "hirelings" is a very real one.

The pastors smile and do the best they can under the circumstances. But their very livelihood depends on satisfying the whims influential church members. This would all be fine if the church were made up of committed Christians. But more and more the lifestyles of the Christian masses are being degraded. Today's statistics show that the lifestyles of Christian are indistinguishable from those of non-Christians. A "popular" minister will not offend. So more and more we see "post-modern" Christians dumbed down to the lowest common denominator. They are given the "OK" to live on the carnal side of their nature. And so the Everlasting Gospel of a holy God is watered down. It is blended with the psychobabble of the motivational speakers of Mammon. These pretenders have infiltrated the church and brought it down to the level of the country club. We are left with a lukewarm insipid syrupy religious stew. Lukewarm "christianity" is considered "normal" nowadays. Nevertheless, it is a mish-mash. Our Savior has told the Laodicean church that "I will spew you out of My mouth". (Rev.3:16) Western Christianity today is already there. The message we broadcast today in the religious bazaars of Mammon is but a pale imitation of the true faith that was once delivered to the saints.

This should not come as a surprise to us. Today as Western Christians we live under the political protection of a merchant world system. Our churches very definitely operate in a religious marketplace. Church membership offers a plethora of church programs, many of which are careful blendings of the holy and the profane. Christian bookstores have become bazaars for books, CD's and DVD's attempting to give spiritual meaning, 'purpose', and motivation to religious customers, most of whom are half asleep and in need of revival. Many who crave this soporific psychological sop are not willing to enter into Blood Covenant with their coming Messiah. They do not **know** the indwelling Christ. Nor have they made Him first in their lives.

As Christian believers the matrix of end-time Babylon is all around us.
The spirit of materialism is trying to get inside of us to dominate us.
And this is what we need to know.
The world they are laying out before us is a fantasy.

It is not real!

Today it has become "normal" for us to "buy" into the socio-religious blend that takes our fancy.
All too often we are inclined to "purchase" our religion at the cheapest possible price.
So the level of Christian commitment we have ended up with in the west is of very low grade.
This is because our relationship with Christ our Lord is lukewarm.

The marketplace of religious beliefs is now operating inside the marketplace of material things.
And the mores of the commercial world have now been

installed inside the House of God.
Jesus told us that we cannot serve two masters.
We cannot serve God and Mammon.

But we are trying to do it!

The mindset inside the western church has slowly changed.

"Blood Covenant" has been replaced by "contract".

The spiritual consequences to this are very disturbing.
The would-be Bride of Christ is not the woman of glory we see in Revelation 12.
Instead she is debased and starting to look like a "material girl".

Of course our commercial contracts bring us some nice things. They keep us comfortable in this world and help us to have a nice day. But our marriage, (whether to our spouse or to Jesus Christ our Bridegroom), should be total and absolute as we see in blood covenant. It should not be brought down to just a "contract for services rendered".

Blood covenant is a two-way relationship. It is also a total commitment unto death. But what do we see in our modern marriage 'contracts'? Instead of being a mutual unconditional blood covenant commitment the marriage covenant is being revised, often in subtle ways. Marriage has effectively been chopped up into two independent conditional one sided 'his and hers' contracts. they are loosely cobbled together in the written and unwritten code of conduct we see in marriage today. Pre-nuptial material contracts are signed by both parties for division of wealth and property should the marriage fail. They are also, (in effect), contracts for "marital services rendered". Each marriage partner comes into the marriage as an independent 'buyer' in a marital marketplace of human bodies and souls. Outwardly the bride and groom pledge to keep covenant "unto death do us part". But the reality nowadays is quite different. Each partner still retains his or her independence inside the marriage. If the "deal" fails to deliver the offended party, perceiving a "raw deal" is able to "walk out" on the basis of "irreconcilable differences". The divorce lawyer, understanding friends, and our indulgent society then help them as they "go through" the divorce.

So much for blood covenant. For many couples entering marriage those blood covenant vows they took are not real. They are relics of an ideal situation, perhaps belonging to people in a former era. They are just another showpiece.

The merchant world uses the same contact law and property law to write up contracts for goods and services rendered. Business deals may also have a 90 day, (or other), cancellation option. Does the marriage "contract" we have today also have a cancellation option? Can the buyer "opt out" if he or she is not satisfied and the spouse does not "meet my needs"?

Apparently so.

This subtle switch of 'contract' in place of 'covenant' has already happened in our marriages.
Is it also happening in our churches?
Could it be happening in our personal relationship with Jesus Christ?

This is a very sobering question. Just what sort of a relationship with Christ have we "bought into"? Is it just "a deal", a "contract" that we might cancel on a whim? Do we 'dump' Christ if we perceive that He "no longer meets my expectations". What if our walk of faith get rough, (as it is in China right now)? How will we react?

Across the waters in the suffering church the Christian life is difficult, and sometimes deadly. But the witness to Yeshua Hamashiach/Jesus Christ goes forth faithfully. 500 of our fellow believers died today. But we never heard about it. It did not make the evening news, or the cable news. Nor was it mentioned from church pulpits.

Western Christians have been blessed. Unfortunately they have allowed themselves to indulge themselves to the full. We as a church have become very spoiled.

So how will the western church respond in the trials to come? What will we do if we are O.B.E., overcome by events? Will we get bent out of shape? Shall we respond in anger or react in savagery when our faith is tested? Shall we join the heathen and rage along with the nations in Edomite anger? Shall we despise our birthright, even as Esau did, for the sake of a mess of pottage and the comforts of the flesh? How many will snarl and beat their fellow servants? How many will despise their relationship with Yeshua/Jesus as a 'raw deal"?

There is much hidden frustration in the Church right now. We may as well face this now, before it is too late for us to repent and change our hearts. How much of this sad/bad countenance is a stubborn or rebellious anger against God? Could our own carnality and self indulgence be the root cause of much of the depression and overweight we see today among western Christians?

Our apostle Paul spoke about a coming "great falling away". How many Christians will "walk out" on their Bridegroom in this coming 'great apostasy'? This is a matter of grave concern. Corrie Ten Boom has presented a very important and sobering message to the Church on this very matter.

It seems that modern western Christian may have been taught, (or may have come to believe), that "grace" means that we are merely passive recipients of this great salvation. Many of us seem to regard salvation as just 'a deal'. A "ticket to heaven" has been provided for us by our "receiving Christ's salvation". It has been purchased for us in full. But here is the question. Can we receive it? And if we can receive it then here is the next question. Can we keep it? Well of course in our own strength we cannot keep the faith. But will we stay around long enough to see God work within us? Shall we see our God "keep" or "preserve" us, even in the midst of trials and tribulations?

ACTIVE LOVE AND DEVOTION.
OUR RESPONSE TO THE LOVE OF THE BRIDEGROOM

Yes, we have a great salvation. And the price of our salvation has been paid. It was purchased in full during Passion Week two millennia ago. We also know that we cannot **earn** this free gift of salvation. We rejoice in the flows of God's grace, and rightly so. Jesus died at Calvary for our sins. He has showered upon us His grace, His "unmerited favor". We have been let off the hook. It is a wonderful reprieve. But is there is more to the covenant than we have been told? Is this escape from eternal punishment all that God's grace will do? Or is there more?

Our apostle Paul exhorted us to,

Philippians 2
12. "....work out your own salvation with fear and trembling,"

And no, he is **not** speaking here about salvation being obtained by our own human effort.
Paul is **not** advocating a of "works" gospel. We know this for a certainty.
Because in the very next verse he goes on to say,
13. "for it is **GOD** who works in you, both to will and to do His good pleasure."

This is active pro-active grace working inside the inner man. The New Covenant is a blood covenant. And yes, it involves a responding action on the part of the Bride. But the energy comes not of ourselves. Rather, the grace comes by the empowering Presence of the indwelling Christ. He has given us His Holy Spirit, and He wants us to be filled to overflowing with Him. The covenant involves **us**. But there is a pre-requisite. We are being called to surrender up our own self life. Our Messiah wants us to let Him in to all the rooms of our soul and psyche. The New Covenant is a two way commitment involving two parties. The Christian faith is ultimately a continuation and an unfolding of the Abrahamic Covenant. It is a two way agreement between YHVH-God and His covenant people, the children of Abraham, Isaac, and Jacob.

So the New Covenant is a mutual two way blood covenant commitment unto death.
It **must** be witnessed by both parties.
Have our pastors and teachers adequately informed us about these things?

Many of us in the west have played around with Christianity. Our Bible is a closed book. Many of us have "played church". A religious smorgasbord has been laid out before us in the religious bazaars. And we are picking and choosing what appeals to us.

This is so sad to report. Most of us in the west have simply not been informed. We do not know that our Christian faith is actually a blood covenant. Few, who call themselves Christians, have even invited Christ into their lives. They do not "know Him" in any real and personal way. We have not yet experienced His inner Life coursing within us. So we drift along in the narcissistic streams of life we see showcased today in the west. Even as Christians we still operate in our own strength and under humanistic guidance. It doesn't work very well. We still lack purpose and meaning in our lives. So we buy all the "self-help" and "human potential" and positive thinking" and "purpose" books in the Christian bookstore to help give our life meaning and "purpose".

The emptiness and the malaise in the western church fails to satisfy. We want more. And we push on to get it. Often we are wont to take "grace" further and further down the river until it becomes "licentiousness". We talk about "personal freedom" for "Me, Myself, and I". But we end up in a wilderness of sin. And like the Lady of Shalott, our love for the coming Bridegroom begins to flicker. While the worthless shepherds smile and take their money today's modern Christians remain starved of the heavenly food. Naturally, they go searching for it. They search for it in all the wrong places. Christians drift on down the river into swamp, a cesspool of "license" and lasciviousness. And in the slough of despair their Christian faith slowly and sadly begins to fade away.

For many in the western merchant church our basic material needs have been met. But our diligence in spiritual matters is just not there. We are inclined to drift in a passive "feed me something I like" sort of faith. Herein lies a great spiritual danger. Christians remain as babes. Swaddled in our material comforts we are 'fat and contented'. There seems to be no need for us to go deeper into the eternal covenant.
So we don't.

Fortunately we serve a God who cares. He loves His covenant people.
And He is going to lead us out of this spiritual quagmire.
He lays out a pathway for us, from
step 1. salvation to
step 2. sanctification to
step 3. glorification.

Our Redeemer takes us on from
step 1. "little children" as babes delighting to be fed the sincere milk of the Word by others, to
step 2. "young men" rejoicing in their strength in the faith, to
step 3. "fathers", concerned for the welfare of the entire global family of faith. (1John 2:12-14)

But most of us in western Christendom are passive in our faith.
We are as little children.
We are still in step 1.
Why is this so?

For new Christians, and many old Christians too, the self-centered 'old man' is still the strongman in our lives. He still wants to rule within us. Under the influence of the world, the flesh, and the Devil, we still give the "old man" the nod to call the shots. And the "old man" will **continue** to rule over the Church until the day comes when we take our faith seriously. We are being drawn into a love relationship. And in that love we shall respond to the Bridegroom. We shall get up from our beds of ease and answer the knock at the door of our heart. And in the devotion we shall invite the indwelling Christ into all the rooms of our spiritual house.

We keep talking about our great salvation as if it were merely a religious purchase deal. We talk and act as if Jesus purchased a ticket to heaven for us and has nothing further for us. But is this true? Could there more to the Covenant? Is there something more involved here, - something we have not been told?

Well of course there certainly is more to the New Covenant.
But do we want to know about these things?
Do we really want that deeper walk in the Spirit of God?

Unfortunately, for most of us, the answer right now is 'no'. We have quite enough 'religion' right now, thank you very much. :-)

Obviously this is an unsatisfactory state of affairs.
And quite clearly it cannot continue on forever.
And it won't.

THE WESTERN CHURCH IS BETROTHED TO HER RETURNING MESSIAH.
SHE IS IN A BLOOD COVENANT RELATIONSHIP WITH HER BRIDEGROOM.
BUT LIKE GOMER SHE HAS GONE OUT INTO THE WORLD TO FIND HER COVERING THERE.
SHE HAS FORGOTTEN HER BRIDEGROOM AND IS STRANGELY UNAWARE OF HER SACRED CALLING.
SHE SLUMBERS IN A SWOON OF PSYCHO-BABEL AND CARNAL SELFISH FANTASIES.
SHE IS ASLEEP. - - - - WHO WILL AWAKEN HER?

This is a very sorry state of affairs in the western church. Over here in the peaceful and pampered western countries our walk with God starts with a 'ticket to heaven'. All too often it stops right there. We let our faith drift. In the narcissistic milieu of our age this has become "normal". We grab our free ticket to heaven and to want nothing more in our relationship with Christ Jesus. We tend to make very little further response to Him in witness to this New Covenant. Like 'Sleeping Beauty' or 'the Lady of Shalott', the Western Church is asleep, and drifting down the river.

The Western Church Slumbers

This idleness is very strange behavior for the Church. She is a 'bride to be'. Does she know what this means? In the relationship with her Bridegroom she is highly privileged. She is especially called to be a witness for the Bridegroom in this world. She has been chosen into a glorious destiny. A holy city of 12 gates awaits her, even the New Jerusalem. It is a huge extended household of many mansions or "dwelling places".

It seems that we have forgotten our glorious calling. We are unaware of our magnificent future. As Christian believers we have become slothful. We have tended to slip off into a certain soporific religious slumber.

What if someone **does** respond to their salvation with enthusiasm? In the 18th century the word "enthusiasm" was a derogatory word used to describe the new Bible believing evangelicals. Their enthusiasm for their Savior seemed strange. It was frowned upon back then. The Church of England padlocked their pews against the preaching of John Wesley. Evangelical fervor was judged as "excessive" or "fanatical" by churchmen of the time. During the Great Awakenings people who began to respond to God's calling in revivals were often told to "settle down".

This still happens today. People who hear God's Word often come under conviction of sin. They may even repent and ask Christ to come into their lives. Some may even be filled with the Holy Spirit and manifest the gifts. People coming into the covenant respond in all parts of their being, and yes, sometimes emotionally. Their subsequent actions often reflect their love for their Savior.

This sort of witness is unsettling to the watching world. Often these responding saints are told to "come back down to earth". The assumption is that they are merely in some sort of temporary "emotional state". Those who respond in this divine romance with some sort of zeal or new commitment may be cautioned, "Don't try to set the world on fire". They may even be reminded that "we are saved by grace" and warned not to 'add works' to God's free gift of salvation.

Is there something wrong with this picture? Christian believers often respond to the indwelling Christ with an entirely new behavior. Is this something we would merely call 'works'? Or is it possible that this is the "normal" response to the wonder of the New Covenant?

Let us return to the picture of the marriage covenant. How about the response of the prospective Bride to the coming of her Bridegroom? This bridal response is part of the covenant story is it not? Is the New Covenant just to be acted out by a single party, the Bridegroom? How about the response of the prospective bride to her Bridegroom? Is the New Covenant just a one way street?

Well the answer to that question is, "Absolutely not!"
In a blood covenant there are **always two parties** involved.

Here is another question that calls for an answer. Why is the Bride of Christ in the west still asleep? Why is "Sleeping Beauty" not awake and preparing herself, even as the 5 wise virgins) did? Why is she not attending to her bridal responsibilities in the covenant? This is something that all good brides do as a matter of course, is it not? Why then, is the Bride of Christ being doped down into abject ecclesiastical passivity, languishing in the pews? Why is she allowing herself to be hypnotized, shoved into the lower hierarchical domination of a religious hierarchy and told "shhhh", "be quiet" and "go back to sleep"? The church as Sleeping Beauty now has the Holy Scriptures and the Holy Spirit is waiting to be asked in. The church emerged from the dark ages over 500 years ago. But she still rests at ease in her glass case of stained glass and crystal. And the toxic apple of false man-made religion is still there in her mouth. Why has she shown so little response to the covenant so far?

OUR CHRISTIAN FAITH IS JUST LIKE MARRIAGE. IT IS A BLOOD COVENANT RELATIONSHIP. IT IS FULL COMMITMENT; EVEN UNTO DEATH.

The whole counsel of the Holy Scriptures bears witness to this fact. The Eternal Covenant of the God of Israel is a blood covenant relationship. It is a commitment unto death enacted in bond of love. It is a two way agreement between two parties, those being our Redeemer, (the Bridegroom), and His Bride, the full Congregation of the God of Israel spread out around the globe.

Let us take a moment here to remember our own wedding, (if we are married). If we take a look at the painting above, we realize that a true bride is not passive. Not at all. She takes a very active and important part in proceedings. She has an essential role of **witness** before Bridegroom and the watching world. Look at her. She is responding to the Presence of her Bridegroom as He approaches. Underneath the signature of the Bridegroom the Bride signs her name. For Christians in the Sudan that act of witness will cost them their lives. Like any bride, the true Bride of Christ, takes a very active part in all the proceedings. She is bringing her witness to her Bridegroom before all who are present and watching. She is vitally, actively, and romantically involved in all of the festivities.

Here is the gist of the matter. The true Bride of Christ loves her Bridegroom! She knows that it may cost her life to sign on the dotted line beneath that of her Bridegroom. But she signs her life away anyway. She is a Bride! She is prepared to testify of her love for her Betrothed, come what may.

And our returning Messiah has a glorious plan for His saints.
Out there in her future is a magnificent destiny that beggars description!

So as the Church comes towards the eventual Marriage Supper of the Lamb she is not to remain just a slave. And she is certainly not just a purchased concubine. Up ahead in a climactic marital ceremony with the returning King the true bride walks in beauty and in grace. She loves her Beloved and is 100% sold out to Him. She has committed herself to Him forever!

This, dear saints, is what the end time drama is all about. Blood covenant commitment unto death is what makes genuine Christianity awesome beyond words. A prospective Bride, God's covenant people, will be the prime witness when the Ancient of Days sits and the courts of heaven are opened. The true church, or Congregation of Israel, will testify before the world of her love for Yeshua Hamashiach/Jesus Christ. And if need be she will bring forth her witness walking through blood and fire, before men and angels. She will demonstrate this marvelous unconditional Agape love her Bridegroom gave her. And she will do so as long as she has breath within her.

Yes, true Christianity goes beyond the salvation "deal". This is a level of faith that is higher than the just a purchase of a cheap "ticket to heaven". Blood covenant issues will come up for consideration in those awesome future days of the final seven years of this age. The New Covenant involves a relationship with God that is far deeper and more awesome than we as westerners know. The blood covenant we have entered into with Jesus Christ goes beyond any business style "contract". It is not a "deal" that is canceled on a whim such as we have in our present day merchant society. Blood covenant is an eternal "blood covenant unto death". It is forever. Blood covenant means "blood for blood". It is like our marriage ceremony. It is "Until death do us part". This, dear saints, is the true "bottom line".

The relationship of true Christians to Christ is just as deep and binding as that of any true bride with her bridegroom. Her level of commitment in the marriage covenant is total. It is absolute. It is not dependent on how the bride-to-be 'feels' about it at the time. The marriage covenant is a blood covenant written in eternity. It is a relationship of total commitment unto death. Marriage was instituted by God. It is a reflection of the higher covenant between YHVH, the God of Abraham, Isaac, and Jacob, and all of His covenant people.

IS THE CHURCH OF JESUS CHRIST A TRUE BRIDE? IS SHE VITALLY INVOLVED IN FAMILY BLOOD COVENANT MATTERS?

OR IS SHE JUST A PURCHASED BUT UNINVOLVED CONCUBINE?

With that picture in mind, here then is the question. Having purchased our salvation with His blood is it likely that our Savior is going to set forth anything different to the patterns He has already instituted in marriage? Are the roles for the Bride of Christ and her Bridegroom to be any different to the pattern God has established in marriage? Is the Bride of Christ passive and out of the loop, as we see in the pre-tribulation rapture scenario? Is Christ, our Bridegroom, going to stroll in, sign and seal the New Covenant all by Himself, and then just go in and "pick up" the bride and carry her off without her knowing what is going on? The end time drama is all about the covenant business of the Most High God. Is the Bride of Christ to be left out of the ceremonies? Is the Wife of the Lamb "out of the loop"?

Messiah is surely coming back again to this earth. He will judge the wicked. Then He will be coming to gather His single Elect and take them off to His mansions in the glory. But how about this pre-tribulation Rapture of an unsuspecting uninvolved 'bride' leaving early without Israel? Does it sound like the way our God does things? Is this all there is to the execution of the New Covenant? Or is there more? Have we heard the 'rest of the story'?

The basic question comes down to this. Is the Bride of Christ merely a "tag along" "do-nothing" sort of woman who waits around waiting to be picked up? Is she just a purchased possession awaiting transport? Is she not personally involved with proceedings? Sort of like a concubine?

Here is another question. Do things just "happen" to this would be bride? Do events happen to her without her knowing about it? Is she surprised by the return of Messiah as if He were a thief in the night? Or is that just the experience of the wicked? Is the woman absent from the final witness and the final showdown of this age?

An awesome Blood Covenant end-time drama in God is up ahead in our future somewhere. It will unfold in the fall feasts during the autumn of some future year. And holy history will come to its glorious climax.

God is still on the throne. He is the Source of all our personal and cultural inspirations. We have inspirations for adventure and inspirations for romance. Who put these holy desires and powerful emotions in the bosom of men and women? Was it not our Creator? Were we not created in His own image? Are we not called into a consecrated relationship characterized by fidelity and devotion in love? Pick up any great novel. In any great adventure or romance do we not see that great love put to the test? Is such an idea really all that strange to us?

ISSUES OF THE END-TIME SEES THE RISING SPECTER OF FEAR.
EVANGELICALS IN THE WESTERN CHURCH BEGIN TO FRET AND WORRY.
THE TRIBULATION PERIOD IS MISREPRESENTED AS "THE WRATH OF GOD". SADLY, BIBLICAL CHRISTIANS ARE ENTERTAINING THOUGHTS OF DESERTION.

Well here we are. In times to come things will change. Our faith and patience could suddenly be put to the test very dramatically. At some point in our lifetime we could find ourselves suddenly thrust into the climax of history.

As we look at the end-time truths outlined in Holy Scripture we can initially become quite alarmed. We might complain, "Nobody warned us!" We might not expect to be challenged to this degree. Some might snarl, "This is a raw deal!" The specter of desertion by a portion of the present day Church is too awful to dwell on. But it is entirely possible that many who call themselves Christians could walk out on God in times to come. Moses warned of this in his closing address to the Church in the wilderness. The Old Testament prophets said that just "a remnant would return". Jesus said that "strait is the gate, and narrow is the way, and few that be that enter therein". Our Apostle Paul warned us that there would be a 'great falling away' from the faith or a 'great apostasy'.

SOME GOOD NEWS FOR THE BRIDE OF CHRIST AS SHE CONTEMPLATES THE "FINAL WITNESS". THE HOLY SPIRIT WILL BE WITH US!

But as Western Christian believers we must not be despondent or disheartened. There is some exceedingly good news to report. Contrary to what we have been told, God, by His Holy Spirit **will** be with us! He will be covering us right through to the very **last day**. That is when our commission, the Great Commission, expires. There will in fact be an End-Time Revival. This will turn out to be a serendipity. We shall find ourselves being drawn, even wooed, into a newer and deeper relationship with YHVH-God, the God of Israel. He is God Almighty, the God who was, is, and evermore shall be. He has expressed Himself abundantly and quite clearly over these past four millennia. His Good News is one of total commitment and loving-kindness. The prophet Hosea said that God and His people, His holy city, were compared to a Husband and His Bride.

We cannot avoid it. End Time Holy history is up there in our future. It will turn out to be a grand adventure. It is also a divine romance. God is in control. He is the Sovereign of the cosmos. And He has written the play ahead of time, even the romance of the ages. Many of these romance elements are seen in the Song of Solomon. Awesome realities are destined to unfold.

Whether we like it or not, the scriptures tell quite a different story to what we have been told. **We**, as Christian believers, are due to go up on the stage of history. This is the divine drama of the latter days. This is the high adventure and the divine romance in God. It goes far beyond the cheap, low grade melodrama churned out by Hollywood. It is a romance and an adventure far more wonderful than what we see today in the depraved and debauched culture of the west. And we shall be there, center stage, before kings and rulers, and before men and angels.

So the would-be Bride of Christ is in the loop here.
And she faces a crucial 'choice'.
What is she going to do?

This will be the burning question in times to come. Is the Church to be unaware and passive in the Rapture, as our present day Bible prophecy teachings have suggested? Will God's faithful witnesses be engaged in cheap, Hollywood style melodrama? Is the end time merely a boring, ho-hum story of survivalist Christians scurrying around like rats after being 'Left Behind'. Or is the truth something entirely different? What does the Bible tell us? Might the true Bride of Christ have a vital, even magnificent, role to play in the end-time drama?

Moses said that God will "call out" His remnant Elect, even "a kingdom of priests and a holy nation." (Exodus 19:6) The Apostle Peter said the same thing. (1Pet.2:9) He echoed the words of Moses saying,

"But you are a chosen generation, a royal priesthood, a holy nation;
  that you should show forth the praises of Him who has called you
  out of darkness into His marvelous Light." (1Pet.2:9)

God will woo His true remnant Elect. He will draw them out of the present day Church and out of present day Israel. His true Bride will come into unity and restoration as a glorious remnant Elect in the crucible of the End-time. (Micah 2:12-13) This will not be a unity established by church-state or church-mammon wheeler dealing. Rather, this peace and unity will come in the refining of the gold the crucible of the end-time. A new blood covenant commitment to Jesus Christ/Yeshua Hamashiah will flow forth as gold. This will be the glory of the end-time, even as pure gold that flows forth from the crucible. Messiah Himself, as the Refiner, will be the author and the finisher of our faith. And He will do this strange work in the drama of the end time. He Himself will work in the hearts of His people. And by this inner working of the New Covenant He will bring about the re-union and restoration of all Israel.

God is at work in His people even now. And in the fullness of time the true Bride of Christ will emerge. She is in the world now. But like Cinderella early in the story she is not too obvious right now. She has been kept out of present day proceedings. But nevertheless, she must go up onto center stage in the times to come. There she will bring her testimony before kings and rulers.
History demands it.

The Church simply cannot be absent or passive in the end-time. She cannot just walk out on her Bride groom like that. She cannot 'go AWOL'. She must be present in the bridal proceedings. She is the key witness and key player in the unfolding of that climactic future time. Holy history will call for her 5th seal testimony. When the four horsemen have finished their ride through modern history and the first four seals and four horsemen have completed their run then the 5th seal 'final witness' of the Church will be called for. This is what has been written in the scriptures. It is an essential part of the story.

So here we see the Bride of Christ. There she stands before the watching world. What will she do? Will she try to escape from her glorious destiny? Or will she stay? Will she testify of her love for her Beloved? Will she sign on the dotted line next to the signature of her Beloved? And will she follow-up on the commitment she made in Word and in deed?

We know the answer. The scriptures are clear. The true Bride of the Lamb will be seen in glory. And the Bride will most certainly bring in her witness (Dan.12). And when all is said and done, a great and glorious company of saints from all races, nations, and tongues will gather before the

throne of God (Rev.7, Rev.20).
What a magnificent witness she will bring!
And what a vision of splendor the watching world will see!

THE BRIDE OF CHRIST ENTERS INTO THE COVENANT IN THE END TIME.
AND SO SHE BECOMES THE WOMAN OF DESTINY JOHN SAW IN REV. 12.

We see the woman of destiny all through the scriptures.
A wonderful picture of her is seen in the Song of Solomon.
We see an overcomer coming to her moment of victory.
The daughters of Jerusalem are amazed.
In wonder they ask,
"Who is this who arises as the dawn,
fair as the moon,
bright and dazzling as the sun,
and as awesome as an army with banners?!"
- Song of Songs 6:8-10

Our Judeo-Christian God/YHVH is our Savior.
He gave His body and His blood for us.
He is worthy or our most ardent zeal and devotion.
He came out of heaven and into our cosmos.
We saw Him in the flesh as Jesus Christ.
He is the Sacrifice Lamb, the Holy One of Israel.
The prophets of Israel saw Him as the Light to the Gentiles.
(Isa.42:6, 49:6, 60:3)
Now, He is the Head of the Church. (1Cor.3:11, 1Tim.2:5)
There is no other.

What can we say about our God? He is the Ancient of Days, the sovereign Ruler who oversees all history? Is He not the

Author of all drama, even the end-time drama? Has He not written "The Play" in which we now finds ourselves taking a part? And didn't He "write the Book" on romance which all others have had to either follow or to twist?

As we come into the final acts of this age we need to ask ourselves some serious questions. God has always called for a witness among men for the great things He has done in His covenant. Shouldn't we expect our God to continue to do this? Shouldn't we expect Him to remain true to His divine character? Isn't this Jesus Christ we see expressed in the Holy Scriptures...

"The same yesterday, today, and forever"?

And our Lord Jesus is a gracious Bridegroom is He not? That being the case, wouldn't it be expected that the Father would call for a witness? And wouldn't He give the Bride an opportunity to have **her say** in the matter?

Let's think about the Bride for a moment. The Bride is coming to love her Bridegroom more and more as we come into the threshold of the Divine Romance and the End-Time Revival. How would **she** be expected to feel about this? Wouldn't a true bride cherish an opportunity to bring her witness before those assembled, even before a cloud of witnesses? Wouldn't a **true bride** actually desire with great passion to testify of the love she has with her beloved? Would she not actually seek an audience before men and the watching angels? And wouldn't her testimony and her bridal witness set her apart from a purchased concubine.

This is sad to have to report but nevertheless true. There are many power hungry Christian pretenders out there who are grasping the authority of Christ. They are in this for the sake of gaining power. And they want the power for themselves. There are also many "gold-digger" or "cargo cult" Christians. These people are like Simon Magus who asked the Apostle Paul to give him the spiritual gifts for him to make money. These are those who follow the way of Balaam for filthy lucre.

Magnificent events are set to unfold the times to come. The final drama will be acted out. And the woman of Revelation 12 will unveiled in all her magnificence. She will be revealed for who she really is. The Bride of Christ is a company of saints destined for a holy city more glorious than we can presently imagine. (Rev. 21)

THE END TIME DRAMA IS A STORY OF TWO WOMEN.
ONE IS THE WOMAN OF WONDER SEEN IN REV. 12.
THE OTHER IS THE HARLOT JOHN SAW IN REV. 17 & 18.

As the end-time drama unfolds it will be plainly seen to be a story of two women. One of them is true and faithful. The other is not. Even in the midst of her trials the true Bride is more precious than rubies. She is quite a bit different from that other woman, the partially committed two-timing harlot. John saw the harlot emerge riding a beast of ten horns. (Revelation 17). Then he saw her destroyed by fire. (Revelation 18)

And so it must come to pass that Christian history will eventually cross a new threshold. Those future days will call for a level of commitment we in the modern or post-modern western church have never seen before.

Our present society loves to ask questions about "feelings". Many a news reporter has asked the question, "How do you feel about that?" Most of our decisions and "choices" revolve around our feelings. And we often make our decisions based on how we answer that question.

OK, let's get "sensitive" here and explore our feelings. How would you feel if - you attended a wedding with a passive non responding bride? What if the girl was given no opportunity to show her face at the ceremonies? What if she refused to turn up to be pictured with her beloved? What if she refused to sign and publicly witness the marriage covenant she had with her bridegroom before God and before men? What if the bridegroom alone signed the marriage document? How would you **feel** if you saw the bridegroom sign the register all by himself? Meanwhile, the would-be bride is just standing idly by, chewing gum and looking out the window. You are at a "wedding". But something is missing. You clearly observe that the woman has been given no chance whatsoever to make a public profession of her love and her commitment to her bridegroom. The bridegroom signs the book then closes it shut. Then snatching his 'tag along bride' he hustles her out the door.

This is a strange sort of wedding isn't it? The wedding ceremony has come to an abrupt end. The show is over. But the bride has not been given a chance to witness or demonstrate the love and commitment she has for her bridegroom!

Well here is the question.
How would you **feel** about that sort of a wedding?
Would that be OK do you think?

Probably not!

OUR BLOOD COVENANT COMMITMENT TO CHRIST IS EXCLUSIVE.
AND OUR DEVOTION TO OUR RETURNING BRIDEGROOM IS TOTAL.

Dear brothers and sisters in Christ. If we are true to our God then our commitment to Him will also be total and absolute. As Christian believers we are all members of the Body of Christ. We have been redeemed. We have been purchased by the shed blood of the Son of God. Our Bridegroom came to this earth 2,000 years ago. He came bearing the bridal price, the gift of our salvation. Now we are saved! We are born again into a new Life in Him. We are His witnesses! Heaven and earth will be watching us as this age comes to its appointed climax.

So how do we respond to this? Do we just slip the New Covenant in our back pocket and forget it? Do we continue to view it as just a "ticket to heaven"? Is this great salvation merely a modern version "indulgence" sold to the crowds by the lukewarm latter day Laodicean church? Do we tell our Savior, 'thanks very much', and then turning our back on Him just walk back out into the world to go about our own business? Is that all that our covenant of salvation with Christ/YHVH involves? Is our relationship with the Bridegroom just a one way street with Him giving

His Life and blood and us just grabbing the "ticket to heaven" and walking off to pursue our own business?

God forbid that we should accept that low grade ecclesiastical "deal". We have a far higher calling and more glorious destiny than that. We are invited into a marvelous Eternal Covenant with the Everlasting God. Our ticket to heaven is very wonderful. But it is just the beginning of our great salvation. It cost the of our Savior and Redeemer Jesus Christ His life blood. He paid the bridal price for our salvation. This is not just a reprieve from hellfire. It is the pathway to eternal glory! Our salvation came to us because of God's love. He was the One who sought us out while we were yet sinners. Are we not to bear witness to Him in this?

God sows His Seed upon the earth and into the lives of His covenant people. There is a harvest. For some it is 30 fold, some 60 fold, and some one hundred fold. Our salvation is just the beginning! Our Lord, our Ishi, Jesus/Yeshua wants to take us further! He plans for us to follow Him. The pathway leads through a strait and difficult gate and along a narrow way. It is not the broad way. And yes, it can be a road of suffering.
But nevertheless, this **is** the road to glory!
It is the Paradise Road.

In the Everlasting Covenant we are His body, - we are His bride. We belong to Him. Are we just to continue on as passive non-responding recipients of His bountiful gift of salvation?
Are we never to grow up into maturity in the faith?
God forbid!

Our God is a gracious God. And yes, it is true that the bridal price has been fully paid. The bill was taken care of by the Bridegroom, our Redeemer. His blood purchased our redemption completely and totally at the cross of Calvary. We cannot add to that blood of atonement. All our human efforts towards that end are fatally flawed and totally useless. The blood He shed for us is holy. In purchasing this great salvation our Savior could receive no help from sinful men. All our attempts to render ourselves acceptable to God based on our own dead works are in vain. As the scriptures state,

"All our righteousness is as filthy rags". -Isa.64:6

"For all have sinned and come short of the glory of God. -Rom.3:23

"Not by works of righteousness which we have done, but according to His mercy, He saved us...." -Titus 3:5

That truth is well established. Indeed, our salvation and our privilege in entering the new covenant was purchased 100% by the atoning blood of our Savior. Jesus Christ, our Redeemer has paid the bridal price for His church. But here is the question that calls out for an answer.
In the outworking of that Eternal Covenant is there not a new life stirring in the heart of the future bride? And in the day in which her witness of the covenant is called for will she not step forward and sign on the dotted line?

These matters should be self-evident. Is it not to be expected that there will be a response by the Bride to this magnificent work of redemption? Is our witness to that purchase agreement of no consequence? Once the bridal price has been paid to the Father of the bride and that legal issue is settled and concluded is that all there is to the Covenant? Is the wedding over? Or does not the bride too have her part to play in the co-signing and the sealing of the covenant?

Well this of course is the essential question and one that our western **Church of Laodicea** has tried to avoid answering. Wouldn't it be expected that the Church, as the Bride of Christ, play an important part in these blood covenant proceedings? After all, will not God's covenant people be present at that magnificent celebration at the end of this present age?
Will she not be present, and robed in glory, at the **Marriage Supper of the Lamb?** And if so, how did she emerge from a wretched and wicked world with such wonderful character?

The Holy Scriptures prophesy that our Bridegroom will sit at table with a glorious bride. She is in the picture, she is in the loop, and she is responsive to her Bridegroom. She is, in fact, a bride who has made herself ready. (Rev.19:7)
Will she not be dressed in white,
even the righteousness of the saints? (Rev.19:8)
Will she not be resplendent with glory,
even of gold refined in the fire? (Zech.13:9, Rev.3:18)

BLOOD COVENANT CHRISTIANITY IS FIRST AND FOREMOST A MATTER OF THE HEART.
AND IT RESPONDS WITH ACTION, FULLY EMBRACING THE END-TIME WITNESS.

AS Christian believers we are not passive in this Eternal Covenant. By the Holy Spirit we are revived. The Life of Christ stirs within us, wooing us, drawing us onward towards the gates of glory. And we awaken, as if from a dream. We may have once been lost and drifting down the river like **the Lady of Shalott** Gomer. But now, in Christ, things have changed. And in His Presence we enter into a serendipity. Oh yes, we now know that as Christian believers coming to the end of the age our lives are in jeopardy. But wonder of wonders! We find that we are now more alive than we have ever been before. In a divine epiphany we become aware of things happening around us that are exciting and unexpected. We have entered into a blood covenant. It is the same Eternal Covenant which Abraham our father knew. And in that blood covenant we discover that we are far from passive. And as the latter days draw near we have a vital and essential role to play. Our witness is being called for. And now we are being beckoned to the stage of history.

BLOOD COVENANT IS A TWO WAY STREET

There are two sides to any blood covenant agreement. This includes the Abrahamic Covenant which is ultimately fulfilled in the New Covenant. In our western church today there is almost no teaching on our faith as a two way blood covenant relationship with God. Instead the New Covenant has been rewritten in the merchant language of contract law. So now the Eternal Covenant with YHVH/Jesus Christ/Yeshua Hamashiach becomes a "deal". In "the deal" we are taught that Jesus gave His all. We put our hand up for a free ticket to heaven.
It's simple! That's all there is to it! (Or so they say.)
This is all very wonderful of course, as far as it goes.

This is the beginning of a wonderful new life in Christ.
But is there **more** to the New Covenant than this?
And if so, have we been told?

In Bible numerics the number "two" is the number of "witness". Similarly, we see this in the marriage procession in our churches to this day. The bride's family sits on one side. The groom's family are on the other. **Both** parties are called to witness the covenant.

When we pray we place both our hands together. It is a sign of the everlasting covenant between ourselves and our God. As we praise God we raise both hands toward heaven signifying that we are a witness to the covenant of Christ. BOTH sides will witness any true covenant. Blood covenant is always a two way accord.
It always has been that way.
And it always will be.

Let us pause and reflect on the wedding ceremony again. A marriage is the climax of a covenant of betrothal. In our western culture is it not fully expected that a bride will go before the watching world in witness to her bridegroom on her special day? Is it not normal procedure for a true bride to publicly bear witness to her marriage covenant? Do we not expect that the bride will co-sign the register with her Bridegroom before all those gathered? And on this day of wonder and weeping is she not declaring her love and her union with the One she loves?

It is in this crucial area that our present Laodicean style church teachings have sold us short. It has become popular to refer to the moment when Jesus cried out from the cross, **"It is finished",** as the completion of the New

Covenant. But wasn't Jesus referring to His finished work of sacrifice on the cross? If the New Covenant had been finished up by our Redeemer 2,000 years ago then why didn't He wrap things up right then and there? Why didn't He emerge from the grave, judge the wicked and glorify His saints at that time? Why has He been waiting around for these past two millennia? If the full burden of the New Covenant was complete back then in 32 A.D. then why didn't He assume His office as Messiah, judge the nations, and establish His Millennial Kingdom right then and there? What was He waiting for?
And what is He waiting for even now?

SIGNED! SEALED! DELIVERED!
THE COVENANT CANNOT BE EXECUTED UNTIL IT HAS BEEN WITNESSED.
IT MUST BE SIGNED AND SEALED BY THE COVENANT PEOPLE OF GOD.
THIS IS NECESSARY BEFORE IT CAN BE DELIVERED.

Is there something that must be seen before the Bridegroom goes off with His Bride? Well in the wedding ceremony we know what that is. The Bride signs the covenant before witnesses. And Jesus Himself told us quite clearly what must happen before he returns.
Here are His very words.
"And this gospel of the kingdom shall be preached in all the world
for a **witness** unto all nations,
and **then** shall the **end** come." (Mat.24:14)

The verse above seems to be a key to the covenant as it applies to the Apocalypse. It seems that the job of witnessing to the nations must be wrapped up **before** this age comes to an end. Only then shall see the second coming of Christ.

So just who did God have in mind to bring this epic **final witness**. Who will be bringing their testimony before kings and rulers and before all nations up until the time of the end? Well it seems that God's covenant people, (His Church), were going to be involved. His Elect would be spreading the Gospel to the ends of the earth. Through an avenue of grace God's Christian, (and returning Jewish), Elect would be divinely enabled to bring their witness to Jesus Christ/Yeshua Hamashiach. Empowerment for witness would come by the inner working of the Holy Spirit. Christ is the head of His church. His people are His body. We live in vital union with Him. Before this age ends the Body of Christ is destined to bring in the final witness. Then comes the return of Messiah and the grand finale to holy history.

The Bride of Christ, even in a time of great travail, is destined to be resplendent in white, even the righteousness of the saints. She will purchase the 'gold refined in the fire' and be covered in the glory of her Father. Her partial blindness will be healed and she will see clearly for the first time. And in the power of this epic and climactic Holy Spirit outpouring the Bride of Christ will come into the End-Time Revival that Joel saw. (Joel 2:28-32) All this will be seen by the watching world.

THE NEW COVENANT IS A BLOOD COVENANT. IT IS THE FULFILLMENT OF THE ABRAHAMIC COVENANT.

The New Covenant we have with Christ began a long time ago. It is a blood covenant. Our Lord Jesus Christ is the Sacrifice Lamb slain from the foundation of the world. - Rev.13:8. The sacrifice of Jesus Christ at Calvary as our Passover Lamb began the fulfillment of the Abrahamic Covenant. Our Gospel came out of the very same blood covenant which YHVH, the God of Israel, cut with Abraham 4,000 years ago. Our spiritual father, Abraham, was present as a **witness** when that original Everlasting and Eternal Covenant with YHVH was cut. The scriptures bear testimony that he was present. - Gen.15. But did he walk it out in his own strength? No, he did not. Abraham's covenant partner, YHVH-God walked through the blood of the covenant for Himself and for his partner Abraham. There was one set of footprints in the blood. Abraham was being carried across a threshold.

This is a magnificent story. God took Abraham out and showed him the stars. He asked Abraham if he could number them. Then He declared to Abraham,
"So shall your descendants be!"
Brothers and sister in Christ, here is something we have yet to realize.
We in the Church, along with returning Judah, are that myriad company of saints!

God respected and honored Abraham. He is our spiritual father. (Gal.3:29) Abraham was a witness to that covenant way back at the beginning. Abraham entered into covenant with YHVH, whose name means 'the God who was, is, and ever more shall be'. When he entered into this two-way blood covenant the saga of the Judeo-Christian people truly began.

Of course Abraham was awed and overwhelmed by it. - Gen.15 God came to Abram as His covenant partner at nightfall. God gave him His Spirit, and part of His name. The "h" in the breath of God turned Abram into Abraham. And to complete the covenant exchange YHVH became the "God of Abraham". Animals were cut right down the middle when that original covenant was "cut". (Gen.15)

Blood is always shed in the making of a blood covenant. This goes beyond "choice". What we are looking at here is total commitment. How can we insist that our teenagers come into responsible commitment if we water down our faith? Unfortunately the "Christianity" we have in the west falls so far short in the commitment department. So much so that Christians refuse to embrace true blood covenant Christianity. Corrie Ten Boom has given us a very important warning about this very thing.

Abraham was God's covenant partner. So too are we. It is by faith in Christ, who is the 'Seed of Abraham' that we come into the family of Abraham, Isaac, and Jacob. This happens when we cry out to God to save us. Our salvation comes by the shed blood of Christ. Christ is the promised Sacrifice Lamb, the Seed of Heaven, and the Seed of Abraham. When we are born again we receive Him into our hearts and into our lives. The indwelling Christ within every true Christian believer is the Seed of Abraham. He is the Seed who brings forth within us our new identity in Christ. And so we become "new creatures".

Is our identity in the Seed of Abraham just a religious matter? With the unfolding of the end time drama we shall discover that the New Covenant is more than this. Both offices of Melchizedek, the political and the religious authorities, the kingdom and priesthood, will be filled by our returning Messiah. He is our High Priest and King of Kings. He is priest and king after the Order of Melchizedek. (Ps.110:4) In covenant with our Messiah we shall bear witness to **both** anointings.

Our Lord Jesus Christ is the Prince of Israel. When we are born again as new creatures we leave our heathen/goyim past. Christ/Mashiach brings us into our new national identity. As incredible as it seems our true Christian identity is in the Commonwealth or Citizenship of Israel. (Eph.2:12-13) As a wild olive branch we are grafted into the olive tree of Israel. (Rom. 11:17)

The Bible also bears witness that toward the end of this age the covenant people of God will preach the 'Gospel of the Kingdom'. This sounds decidedly political. So we know that the coming of Christ as Messiah is more than just a religious matter. And as we can readily see from the apocalyptic books of Daniel and Revelation the reality of earthly politics will definitely be involved. In fact the nations will be raging. King David wrote a song about this 3,000 years ago. (Ps.2)

This still sounds strange to us. But it is in the Seed of Abraham, not just our national or racial seed, that we find our true eternal identity. Jesus Christ entered His city of Jerusalem 2,000 years ago riding on a donkey. As our Kinsman Redeemer came bearing the bridal price. And that price was measured out in His blood. He is destined to be the banner and standard for the peoples. In Him we find the only esteem we shall ever need. - Mat.13:44 He has left us a great treasure hidden in a field. In Him we begin to discover, and come to possess, our inheritance. In the covenant the Testator in His death has left us great expectations. He has left us an eternal dwelling place in His Kingdom, and mansions of glory.

As we have seen, the saga of the redemption of this planet and its people is very much a family business. It is the family business of the children of Abraham, Isaac and Jacob. As the scriptures testify,

"If ye be Christ's then are ye Abraham's seed
and heirs according to the promise". (Gal.3:29)

THE NEW COVENANT CHRIST MAKES WITH INDIVIDUALS WILL GO ON
TO FULFILL THE OLD COVENANT GOD MADE WITH THE NATION OF ISRAEL.

Contrary to what we have been told, God is not through with the nation of Israel. He will use the New Covenant he makes within human hearts to fulfill the Old Covenant He made with the Nation of Israel. This is truly amazing! The New Covenant is the outworking of the Old Covenant through the promised Seed of Abraham. Then God turns around and uses the New Covenant He makes within individual hearts to restore the Old Covenant He made with the nation of Israel. Wrapped up in this restoration of Israel is the promised great Light to the Gentiles. bringing salvation to the ends of the earth. - Isa.49:6 In such a manner YHVH's grand restoration project will come full circle.

So just how will the New Covenant we have in Christ go on beyond the lives of individuals to restore the nation of Israel? God is obviously planning a full and total restoration here! Just how does He propose to do this?

Well His plan here is no secret.
Repeatedly, back in the Old Testament, God has said He would restore the nation of Israel. Here in the verses below we see just how He will go about it.

Jeremiah 31:31-34
31. "Behold, the days are coming, says the Lord, when I will make a **new covenant** with the house of Israel and with the house of Judah-- 32. not according to the covenant that I made with their fathers in the day that I took them by the hand to lead them out of the land of Egypt, My covenant which they broke, though I was a husband to them, says the Lord. 33. But **this is the covenant** that I will make with the house of Israel after those days, says the Lord:
I will put My law in their minds, and write it on their hearts;
and I will be their God, and they shall be My people."

The New Covenant we have in the Church/Ecclesia/Congregation of Christ is therefore the fulfillment of the Abrahamic Covenant. -Gen. 15 It is a blood covenant relationship based on a great salvation that comes in by grace through faith in the blood of the promised Sacrifice Lamb. Indeed our Lord Jesus Christ is the Seed of Abraham. He came in the flesh as that ultimate Sacrifice Lamb. He shed His blood "giving His life as a ransom for many". (Mat:20:28) The task of bearing witness to His great salvation and His righteous rule within men's hearts, would go out beyond the borders of Israel. It would involve the preaching of this "Good News"/Gospel of salvation to all nations. The Light went out to the gentiles in an enormous worldwide missionary outreach. It would bring these new believers into the Commonwealth of Israel. (Eph.2:12-13) This witness was going out beyond the DNA genetic riverbed of national/racial Israel. Like the Jordan River, the Seed of Israel would overflow national riverbanks of Israel all the days of the harvest. (Josh 3:15) These waters of Life would go out as a flood to the surrounding heathen gentile nations. Ultimately it would bring in a magnificent harvest. The Seed of Abraham, Jesus our Savior, would enter into humble human hearts out among the nations. The Gospel is even now being preached to the ends of the earth.

Jesus Christ/Yeshua Hamashiach is Israel's "Light to the Gentiles". (Isa.42:6-7) The the end of the story will see the fullness of the Gentiles will be brought in. Then National Israel will be saved even as Jerusalem is surrounded by the armies of the nations at the Battle of Armageddon. (Joel 2:28-32) The royal Jewish house of Judah will be saved to rejoin the wider Commonwealth of Israel. Both houses will be re-united together as one single remnant Elect. (Rom.11) The throne of David will be restored by the returning Christ. He is the Lion of the Tribe of Judah (Rev.5:5) and our coming Messiah. (Zech.12:7-13:1)

"And so all Israel shall be saved".-Rom.11:26

AT PENTECOST THE COVENANT GOD MADE WITH ISRAEL OVERFLOWED INTO THE GENTILE

NATIONS. THE HOLY SPIRIT OUTPOURING WILL CONTINUE TO POWER UP AND COME TO A GLORIOUS CLIMAX IN THE END TIME.

The witness to the gentiles began on the Day of Pentecost in that epic summer of 32 A.D. There were 120 committed Jewish saints in that upper room when the Holy Spirit fell. On that day the witness went out mightily into the city of Jerusalem. When Peter preached there were 3,000 saved. But that was just the beginning. That job of witness, of making disciples of all nations, races and tongues was going to take some time. Christ is our Head. We are His body, His church the "ekklesia" or "called out" congregation of saints. His witness flows through us and out to the watching world. We are living epistles, read of men, written not with ink but by the Spirit of the Living God. -see 2Cor.3:3 Jesus said that He would **not** be concluding this present age, or "generation" until that task of witness was completed. Only then would the end come.

We now live and witness in the age of the gospel. The gentile church expansion went out from the early first century Jewish church in Jerusalem. From Jerusalem it went on to Judea. From Antioch the main bulk swung westwards into Asia Minor. Today it extends out towards the uttermost parts of the earth. That mission is not finished. It will continue throughout the final seven years of this age until the awesome blow-out climax of this age at the 6th seal. -Joel 2:28-32

GOD'S PEOPLE ARE NOT JUST PASSIVE RECIPIENTS.
A TRUE BRIDE IS VITALLY INVOLVED IN WITNESS

TO THE COVENANT SHE HAS MADE WITH THE BRIDEGROOM.

So we as Christian believers are not passive in the covenant. We are His witnesses.
Our Christian witness to the Good News is **our** side of the covenant.
This response we have to the indwelling Christ comes by a ministry of His divine grace. It is not a matter of our "works". Our witness to His Great Salvation flows out of the blessings of the covenant. Our power to witness comes as we open our hearts to Him. And our witness is a response He produces in us by His Holy Spirit. It is a response to His wooing.
It is a response to His love.
This is the "rest of the story".

For how long will this witness period of the Great Commission, (-Mat.28:18-20) be expected to continue? An obscure prophecy in Hosea suggests that the final climactic revival would come 2 millennia of biblical (360 day) years from the last "cutting" prophetic words of God. (-Hos.6:1-2) These cutting words were given in the Olivet discourse in the springtime of 32 A.D..

So why do we assume that the covenant between Christ and His people was all finished 2,000 years ago at the cross? We hear that a lot from the pulpits. Do we like it that way? If so, why? Is it because we only wish to bother ourselves with the legality of **our** own personal ticket to heaven?

What about our corporate collective identity as the congregation of the elect, the called, the chosen, and the faithful? Are we not individually just one of many saints, a glorious company of God, from all nations and from all historical periods? Do we have a sense of the wonder and the splendor of that great company of which we are members? -Heb. 11:1-12:6 Are we the final runners out on a grand relay race? And will our race take us to that glorious finish line? Are we readying ourselves spiritually to run that race? -Rev.3:18. Is there not a world to win? Do we, as the congregation of saints,

"....have promises to keep,
And miles to go before we sleep"?
-Robert Frost

HAS THE NEW COVENANT BEEN FINALIZED? HAS IT BEEN SIGNED AND SEALED? IS IT READY FOR EXECUTION/DELIVERY RIGHT NOW?

Here is another issue. Is it possible we could be members of the Laodicean church? Many narcissistic Christians are satisfied with their Christianity as a legal matter, a ticket to heaven and little else. But are we sure that our own personal "deal" or "contract" with Jesus is all signed, sealed and ready to be delivered?
Does our decision to follow Christ "finish" our faith?
Or is being "born again" (-John 3:3-7) just the beginning of our walk? If our Ishi/Beloved, Jesus Christ the "author and **finisher** of our faith" (-Heb.12:2) can we truthfully say that His work in us is finished?

HISTORY AWAITS THE WITNESS OF THE CHURCH AS WE COME TO THE CLIMAX OF THE AGE.

Here is another consideration. Is there not going to be an endtime apostasy, a great "falling away" from the faith by many in the end time drama? -2Thes.2:3
Didn't Jesus exhort us to patience when He said,
"He who endures to the end, shall be saved?" -Mat.24:13

And have we, as the collective covenant people of God, completed our role of witnessing the good news of our Lord Jesus Christ to the ends of the earth?
Have we "signed on" to all His wonderful truths?
Have we witnessed and testified to all His power,
all His glory, and all His victory?
Even His victory over death?
Has holy history for this age been wrapped up?
Has the Great Commission been completed?
Has the Gospel been preached to the ends of the earth?-Mat. 24:14
Have we seen all the "greater works" of the Holy Spirit?-Joel 2:28-32
Has the House of David and the whole Jewish house of Judah
repented and been saved?-Zech.12:10-13:1
Has the city of Jerusalem been delivered from the armies of the nations mustered at Armageddon?-Zech 12:1-9
Has the last lost sheep of the House of Israel been found? - Mat.15:24
Has the pilgrim family of Abraham (-Gal.3:29)
come to the end of their long Journey from Ur?
Have all the covenant people of YHVH, finally come home?
Have they arrived there before the throne,
singing the song of Moses,
before the crystal sea? - Rev.15:2-4

What if the answers to the above questions are "no"? Well then we must conclude, that even though we may be committed Christians individually, the new covenant we have collectively "cut" with the Redeemer is still unsealed. The marriage covenant which we, the corporate Judeo-Christian Elect, have with the Bridegroom, has not yet been fully witnessed. It has not been signed. As committed partners in a blood covenant relationship with God our role has not yet played out to its conclusion. Indeed holy history awaits the completion of our signature and our witness on **all** its points.

**THE NEW COVENANT WILL BE SEALED FOR THE COURTS OF HEAVEN
AND READY FOR EXECUTION AT A CERTAIN FUTURE TIME IN HOLY HISTORY.**

When will this final signature and the sealing of the New Covenant occur? This momentous event will occur after the four horsemen have exhausted all their strength. This final signing and sealing of the new covenant by God's people will indeed happen just as prophesied. God's elect will indeed sign and seal the covenant and bring it to closure. But when?

The scriptures show us quite clearly that this climactic apex of Christian witness will occur at the 5th seal. -Rev. 6:9-11, Joel 2:28-32 This corresponds to the final half of the 70th week of Daniel. The time allotted by God for this final witness is the final three and one half years of this age. Indeed this epic and climactic signing and sealing of the everlasting covenant by the saints is what the 5th seal witness is all about. The 6th seal follows with the sign of Christ appearing in the heavens under a darkened sun and a bloody moon. -Rev.6:9-12 At this point, the Second

Coming of Christ and the Resurrection-Rapture is imminent.

Dear saints, we may not like this scenario at all. But this is what has been written in the Holy Scriptures. It must be this way.
Why?
Because we are not passive in our relationship with Christ. And we cannot be passive, or absent, in the end time. We, after all, are the covenant people of God. The fire of His love burns within the hearts of those who know Him. -Luke 24:32 It is a fire that cannot be extinguished. (Jer.20:9, Song of Songs 8:6) Even the cosmos, the creation no less, awaits our final witness and glorification. The earth and the ecosystem is groaning, awaiting its restoration.

"For the earnest expectation of the creation, eagerly awaits the revealing of the sons of God."- Rom.8:19

THE GRAND FINALE TO HOLY HISTORY FOR THIS AGE.

Just like in the classic fireworks festival, there is to be a similar grand finale at the end of this age. The climax or peak of the Holy Spirit outpouring will be seen at the end of this age. - Joel 2:28-32 The close of this age will see the completion of the witness of the church. And the 6th seal will follow with the cosmic disturbances and the appearance of the sign of the Son of Man in the heavens.- Mat.24:29-31 and Rev.6:12-17. At His glorious second coming the Holy Spirit outpouring will climax at that time. And the saints will go out in a blaze of glory. They will find themselves caught up in a magnificent deliverance, -Micah

2:12-13; even as the sun turns to darkness, the moon turns to blood, and the stars fall.-Joel 2:28-32

THE BRIDAL PRICE:
AND OUR RESPONSE.

The bridal price, the price of our redemption, was enormous.
God Himself took on flesh, carried our sin, and purchased our salvation.
He sent the Holy Spirit who sanctifies us from within into the likeness of Christ.
He empowers us to do His wonderful work.
Our privileges and responsibilities are far from over. -Mat.28:18-20.
We shall also have responsibilities in the Millennial Kingdom to come. -2Cor.2:11-12, Rev. 20:4-6.
That will continue on in the new heavens and new earth.

Are we aware of the glorious destiny God has planned for us? We shall go out beyond this present earthly station into realms of splendor far beyond description. -Rev.21

THE WESTERN CHURCH AT THIS POINT IN TIME IS THE RELUCTANT AND HALF-ASLEEP BRIDE OF CHRIST.

So.
All that being understood.
Why all this reluctance to co-sign the new covenant as bridal witness alongside the signature of our Bridegroom? Is the Western Church a 'runaway bride'? When we take communion do we not sit down at the communion table

and drink His cup fully betrothing ourselves to Him? Do we
not sup with Him, even as David, "in the presence of our
enemies"? -Psalm 23
Why all this fog of forgetfulness in the rich western church
today concerning what the cup of Christ really means?
Why all this malaise?

Here we are, camped out once more,
by the rivers of Babylon.
And our harps hang in the willows,
as they did long ago.
We remember, and we long for,
a Holy City yet unseen.

Shall we ever see that City?
Shall we enter through its gates?
Gates of righteousness and mercy?
Shall we see the vision splendid?

Oh yes, we shall arrive at last;
What a Day that will be!
When "the ransomed of the Lord shall return,
And come with singing unto Zion,
And everlasting joy,
shall be upon their heads".- Isa.35:10

We have been ransomed, redeemed, bought back,
purchased at an awesome price. -1Cor.6:20
What is our response to this great salvation?
Do we just work and play, watch the ballgame and the
soaps on TV, talk with our stockbroker, attend church, and
wait around for the rapture?
Is the bride of Christ, passive in the covenant?
Are we, as the bride of Christ merely "purchased goods",

awaiting shipment to an upscale piece of property in the New Jerusalem?

Hardly.

THE NEW COVENANT AND THE HEBREW/WESTERN WEDDING BETROTHAL.
THE BRIDE'S WITNESS, HER SIGNATURE, AND HER SEAL ARE THERE ON THE RECORD.
THESE ARE ALL ESSENTIAL PARTS OF A TRUE MARRIAGE.

The New Covenant opens with a betrothal. And in any true Judeo-Christian marriage betrothal the bride always signs the register. She will be present and bear witness to her marriage covenant. If her signature of witness is not inscribed on the document beneath that of or the Bridegroom then such a document cannot be sealed and consummated. And as a matter of law the arrangement would not be a legitimate marriage. Without her witness it will fail to bring forth the glorious consummation that a true bride would long for.

Why is an unwitnessed marriage covenant of no value? Because without her signature such a consort would be showing her indifference to her consort. She would not have publicly declared **marriage** to the man before God and men. It would be obvious to all that she was there as part of some sort of undeclared sex deal. Without the bridal statement of total commitment, the relationship would not be a marriage at all. Without total spiritual commitment expressed by **both** parties there would only be weak fleshly and material bonds holding the two together. And without that vital commitment the woman would not be a true bride.

If she was not a bride then what might she be? In the typology she might be a bond slave or the consort of what we might term nowadays a "sugar daddy". At best she could be a "common law" wife. Otherwise she might be a "mistress", or a concubine. Perhaps she might be just out to enjoy the physical blessings the Bridegroom brings, and only for a season here below as well as their ticket to heaven in the sweet by and by. (And sadly, that is all that some Christians want of God.) But in such an uncovenanted earthy relationship where would be the romance and the adventure? The Bridegroom would not really have her heart. And she would not really have experienced the splendor of His love. She would not "know Him". Nor would her heart be committed to go with him through the Valley of Decision and beyond, into that magnificent Marriage Supper that awaits them. As a concubine she would be passive and unresponsive to all this romance and drama. Instead of being a true bride she would out of the loop. She would merely be an indigent or indifferent spectator to an unwitnessed, one-sided, half-baked, incomplete, unfulfilled covenant.

MARRIAGE IS MORE THAN JUST A PURCHASE AGREEMENT OF A WOMAN BY A MAN.
IN SUCH A DEAL THE MAN WOULD BE PIMPING FOR HIMSELF.
AND THE WOMAN WOULD BE A CALL GIRL, A HARLOT, OR A CONCUBINE.
DEVOTION TO CHRIST DRAWS US INTO A LOVE RELATIONSHIP.

IT IS A TWO-WAY BLOOD COVENANT COMMITMENT "UNTO DEATH".

Is the marriage covenant the payment of the bridal price and nothing else?
If that were the case then such a transaction would be a unilateral one on the part of the bridegroom. It would then become merely a contract for delivery of the young woman into his household service. If she were not called upon to give her consent or witness then the coupling would be organized **around** her but not **with** her. We saw this very scenario played out in that wonderful musical, "Fiddler on the Roof". Such a bridal purchase/dowry deal was contracted between the prospective bridegroom and the father of the bride. The woman in question was not involved. The dowry agreement was consummated, declared to be a done deal, and celebrated before the actual wedding was to take place. But it was a hollow and empty affair. The bride-to-be was not invited into the proceedings. There was no **consent and no witness** to the covenant. Nor was there a declaration of love by the girl to follow up on that arrangement for a marriage conducted through third parties.

The result was quite predictable and awful.
There was no wedding; ... and no marriage supper.

THE CHURCH, THE CALLED OUT CONGREGATION OF CHRIST.
IS SHE A TRUE BRIDE?
OR IS SHE JUST A PASSIVE CONCUBINE WITH A PURCHASE/INVOICE TICKET TO HEAVEN?

We all enjoy going to weddings. And we are moved to see the bride and groom make their vows. They totally commit themselves to each other in a blood covenant unto death. And they do this before a host of witnesses. This is where the handkerchiefs come out and the tears are brushed aside. It is a special time of consecration rarely seen in our society. But what if we were to attend a wedding where that did not happen?

OK, let us lay out the scene here. What if the man declared himself willing and paid his dowry price. But the girl was absent from the proceedings? How would it be if you attended a "wedding" where the "bride's" witness and consent was not considered necessary at all? The bridegroom was there. And he proceeded to sign an agreement between just himself and the father of the girl? How would that go down?

In some cultures, sometimes in the Islamic world and in pagan cultures, this very thing happens. The "bride" is not given a chance to respond. Her bridal and marital response is not considered an issue at all. Effectively the man is signing an invoice for the delivery of the girl. She is being purchased and brought into his household service for sexual consort, child bearing, and housekeeping. He signs the agreement for her unilaterally just as he would sign a receipt for a bond slave, or for cattle. The contract would be little more than a bill of lading for the arrival of the man's property, for promised goods. The price paid for her would not be a dowry but only a payment for consort. In such a scenario the girl's consent would not be in the picture. Her response would be assumed and by-passed in the celebration. The woman would be just a passive third party to a financial deal.

Of course this would be preposterous. This would be a far cry from our Judeo-Christian standard for marriage. In such a one sided contract the girl in question would not truly be the covenanted wife of the bridegroom. At best, she would be like Gomer, the unfaithful wife of Hosea, after he purchased her in a slave market. At that stage she would merely be a purchased bond slave or handmaiden.

Is this a far as the relationship will go?
That, dear saints, is the big question for the western church.
Most Christians today are living on the carnal side of their nature.
They have only experienced the lower levels of love, even eros.

But as with Gomer, perhaps the church will go through the Valley of Achor, or tribulation.
And like Gomer, perhaps the church may begin to sing, and to remember her Betrothed.
She may even cease from calling Him "Lord" and start to call Him "Ishi", or "Beloved".
And perhaps in the Valley of Achor the church may learn to love unconditionally,
Even with that higher level of "agape love".

GOMER, THE UNCOMMITTED AND WAYWARD WIFE OF THE PROPHET HOSEA:
IS SHE A 'TYPE' OF THE ESTABLISHED CHRISTIAN CHURCH?

Is the scriptures we read an amazing love story. It is the saga of Hosea and his wayward wife Gomer. It has been rightly interpreted as a prophecy for national Israel. But have we perhaps been inadequately informed about the full extent of this prophecy? Is this Hosea and Gomer story also a prophecy of the wayward compromised western Church?

Gomer would not settle down and commit to her husband, Hosea. Her wanton eyes took in the baubles of the world and she was drawn to secular champions, princes of Rome and the ones that followed. And so Gomer drifted away from her true husband, bringing him terrible grief. She spent many years wandering in the world, committing adultery with her princely lovers. But as the story unfolds she is betrayed by all of them. Her final fling was the worst of all. And eventually Hosea finds his beloved lost wife. He finds her in a slave market. -Hos. 3:1-2

This is just the way it has been, (and will be again), for YHVH the God of Israel with His wayward people. Hosea purchased his wife Gomer back to himself. He redeemed her, buying her from her taskmasters for 15 pieces of silver. At that stage she is purchased goods... and nothing more.

Is this beginning to ring a bell with us?

At that time Gomer had been redeemed. She was certainly very grateful to her Bridegroom for saving her. But she had not yet really learned to love Him as Her Betrothed in any deep and committed sort of a way. Isn't that like us in the western Church today?

Gomer had initially called her betrothed "Baali" or "My Lord". She did not yet know him as "Ishi" or "Beloved". -Hos.2:16 She only really learned to love Him when she

made her deeper discoveries. She found her 'Ishi', and fell in love with him in the Valley of Achor (tribulation). - Hos.2:15
She found her Beloved, and would not let Him go. - Song of Songs 3:4 Is that a prophetic picture of God's Judeo-Christian covenant people? Is this a snapshot of what they will experience in the end time?

HAS THE CHURCH ENTERED INTO COMMUNION WITH GOD?
HAS SHE LEARNED TO RESPOND TO HIS LOVE?

Is the receiving of the bridal purchase all that Jesus/Yeshua has for His church?
Because that is what is being taught from the pulpits of the untried untested pampered western church. The bridal purchase of Christ for His congregation is being sold on the streets as merely a free ticket to heaven. From a legal standpoint this is a wonderful start. But do we say, "That's all folks!?"

Let's think this over for a bit. If the would-be-bride does not go on to respond in love to the bridal purchase offer and respond by fully committing herself to him alone then who is she? She remains just an **object** of God's love. She is just a young thing who has not yet come into her character. She has not gone on further to become a **responder** to love. She does not **KNOW HIM**! If there is no ensuing love relationship beyond the purchase agreement then she merely continues on as chattel;
She is "purchased goods".
She remains passive in the covenant.
She does nothing.
She is "out of the loop".

DOES THE NON-RESPONDING CHURCH HAVE AMNESIA?
DOES THE BRIDE REALIZE WHO SHE IS?

Will she go on to the glorious consummation? Maybe.
If she is brought to a place where she comes to remember.
Remember the Covenant.
And remembers who she really is.

But what if she is comfortable and content with her "ticket to heaven".
What if she wishes to go no further in the relationship than that?
Perhaps this "easy believism" would be easy for her and she would remain popular with her friends.
But in such a scenario is she really and truly a called out bride?

It is questionable.

She not fully testified publicly of her love for her Redeemer/Bridegroom.

THE BELOVED IS THE DIVINE VISITOR.
HE IS KNOCKING AT THE DOOR OF OUR HEARTS.
HE WANTS TO COME INTO OUR LIVES AND TALK WITH US.
HOW SHALL WE RESPOND?

In the Song of Songs, the Shulamite had a second disturbing dream. In this dream her Beloved came knocking at the door. But she was too pre-occupied with her own comfort to respond. She does not get up to open to Him. He disappears. As the story unfolds she finally leaves her house of ease and goes out looking for Him. She enters into some trials and tribulations. She is struck by the watchmen of the city. They take away her veil. In all of this she never ceases from seeking and testifying of her absent Shepherd lover. -Song of Solomon 5:2-8 Why was she struck by the watchmen? In her self absorbed state the Shulamite had lost her honor in the eyes of the world.

The western church today is in that very same situation. She is comfortable. She knows that her Betrothed is "out there somewhere". Meanwhile she is preoccupied with herself, engaging in a fruitless narcissistic pursuit of "self esteem". Yet she never finds happiness and satisfaction. Why is this so?

The answer is simple. True happiness lies in the very devotion she and her psychologist friends have studiously avoided. She is the bride of Christ. Her true esteem is only to be found **in Him!**

The western church is not like that today. What is wrong with us? Why all this spiritual indifference to the blood Covenant Christianity. Is this aversion to intimacy with our Betrothed just part of the "grace" which our Bridegroom bestows on us?
God forbid!

Brothers and sisters, this is where the worldly religion of cheap, unilateral, merchant contract law has led us. In our flight from **blood covenant** we have become prisoners in a materialistic world of mundane objects. The people of God are still just rendered as "objects" of God's love. They are not yet functioning "participants" in His love. A cheap gospel without any preparation for a deeper subsequent commitment to Christ is just another evangelical form of the "indulgence" of the type the medieval Roman church sold to the peasants in the Middle Ages. Christians continue to be ushered away from the great devotion. And they have still not discovered the true Agape love in Christ.

Is the church today still boxed up by Nicolaitan religious powers? Have we really come all that far from the religion of the peasants in the middle ages? How many evangelical Christians today are still dependent on intermediaries between them and Jesus Christ? For most of us we still need to be spoon-fed the Word of God for one hour on Sunday. We lack a daily personal walk with God. And milk, not meat, is all that most of us desire or can handle. Even in our elder years we continue on as spiritual "children". (1 John 2:1-18) In our church life we continue to content ourselves with being mere spectators to bold motivational speeches by crusaders and being patrons to loud musical concerts. This sweet soporific "poisoned apple" of marketplace religion leaves the church "cold", - just as we find her today.
And that is how she remains; a non-responsive "Sleeping Beauty".

THE CRISIS OF THE CHURCH IN THE END TIME DRAMA.

Our western culture has many stories of the central character being alienated and cut out of the ceremonies. This is the case with the "Ugly Duckling".
He doesn't know who he really is;
- Until the end of the story.

In the story of Cinderella her stepsisters cut her out of the climactic gala events.
They compromise and connive and for their own pride of place in the ball.
The would-be-princess is hidden away from the returning Prince.
She sits in the cinders in alienation and tribulation.
But all of that will change,

- in the midnight hour.

If the church has being alienated like Cinderella, or is doped and "out of it" like Sleeping Beauty", is she just a victim here? Or might she have brought some of this upon herself? We in the western church, the former center of Christendom, have accepted very little responsibility in the covenant with our God, especially with the gospel. Only 5% of our church budgets go to missions. Like Cinderella we have played in the dirt of sin. And like Sleeping Beauty we continue to accept the poisoned apple of pre-packaged formula religion. This has effectively doped us, put us to sleep, and kept us "quiet" for the ruling elites. But our returning Prince, our Messiah, is coming.

At midnight the shout of the friend of the Bridegroom will be heard. (Mat.25:6)
We shall be awakened, - at the midnight cry.
In the darkness the saints shall get up to trim and fill their lamps.
Do we have the oil?

OUR PREPARATION IN THE SPIRIT.
FINDING THE OIL FOR THE COMING NIGHT.

Do we take our personal faith seriously?
Do we remember the Great Commission?
Do we seek the fullness of the Holy Spirit?
Or are we content with the pursuit of our own happiness?

Dear saints, this state of affairs cannot last much longer.
History will come to a climax.
And like it or not, we are right in the middle of it.

THE CALL TO BLOOD COVENANT COMMITMENT WITH JESUS CHRIST/YESHUA HAMASHIACH

Our relationship with Jesus Christ is a blood covenant relationship. We have avoided that and accepted a cartload of cheap imitations in its place. In the ensuing vacuum we seek deep purpose in our lives from many other substitutes. We seek that deeper meaning to life in all the wrong places; We seek meaningful blood covenant relationships in our careers, in Freemasonry, in fraternities and sororities, in military and warrior gatherings of radical nationalism. Spectator sport has reached cultic levels and riots break out at football and soccer matches. We seek blood covenant in racism, in royalty and rock star worship, in the business cult worship of the golden calf/bull market of mammon on Wall Street. We seek it in the peasant cult of communism, in religious cults, in the eco-cults following the shamans of the goddess Gaia around "Mother Earth". The sexual cults of Hollywood and pornography on the internet are swallowing souls by the millions. Our children more than ever, are seeking deeper and more meaningful blood covenant relationship in sexual affairs, in street gangs, in drugs, in body piercing and the tattoo parlors. All this while the established western church slips away into the slime pits of personality cults, feminism and homosexuality.

The God we love, (who deserves first place), we no longer seem to remember.

Is this world of mammon all there is? The scriptures testify that this present age of human government will lead on towards a general state of apostasy. Those called of God will even enter into a covenant by with a false messiah. - John 5:43, Dan.9:27 Then history will come unglued. It will destabilize violently in a raging of nations. Only the return of the Messiah will save this world from utter destruction.- Mat.24:22 At a certain time in future history Christ will return to judge the nations and to establish His Millennial Kingdom. -Isa.40. Will He be welcomed by the powers of this world? Not at all. The nations are even now conspiring and raging against His coming rule. King David wrote a Psalm about the last days conspiracy of secular humanism and religious humanism a full 3000 years ago. -Ps.2. Eventually the powers of this world will gather their armies against Jerusalem on the plain of Armageddon in northern Israel.

What if our Deliverer comes later than we have been told? What if future church history, like the first three centuries, calls for our witness to the Kingdom of Jesus Christ? What form might our bridal witness take then?
Will pressure be put on us to compromise our faith in Him? Have we considered this?
Like the Shulamite, are we due for some adventures?
And like Gomer, shall we find ourselves falling in love with our Beloved,
even in the Valley of Achor/Tribulation?-Hos.2:15

BLOOD COVENANT CHRISTIANITY = AGAPE LOVE OF GOD

True agape love means total exclusive commitment. We are called to holiness. As the scriptures say,
10:21 You cannot drink from the cup of the Lord and from the cup of demons.
You cannot eat at the Lord's Table and at the table of demons, too.
- 1Cor. 10:21

Our God is calling us to Him. Future holy history will see to it. Our God is also calling us to that divine romance of which the Shulamite in the Song of Solomon testified,

"Set me like a seal over your heart, As a seal upon your arm.
For love is as strong as death,
And jealousy is as cruel as the grave.

Its flashes are flashes of fire,
A most vehement flame,
The very fire of the Lord"
-Song of Songs 8:6

In the Jewish Wedding Betrothal ceremony the prospective bridegroom presents the cup of wine before the one he loves and hopes to marry. She either drinks from his cup signaling her agreement to the betrothal; or she gets up and leaves. The true bride will accept His cup of betrothal. As she takes His cup, she remembers Him. And she drinks "all of it".-Mat.26:27-28. Blood covenant cuts both ways. Both give themselves totally to each other, to the extent of all they own, - and to the extent of their very lives. Herein lies the mystery of a true and happy marriage.

And for the church/ecclesia coming into union with Yeshua/Jesus herein is also found the "mystery of godliness" in Christ Jesus.-1Tim.3:16

Even through all her trials and tribulations, His betrothed bride, remains loyal and true. Like the Shulamite in the Song of Songs she has resisted the seductions of the "man of the world" (King Solomon). She ignores the enticements of his property, his power, his pomp and his pageantry. She is unaffected by the peer pressure of hundreds of other wives and concubines, those "daughters of Jerusalem", in the harem of King Solomon. She has rejected their temptations. How?

Because of the One to Whom she is betrothed. She cannot forget her absent Shepherd lover. She loves him. And she knows that He will come for her.

Meanwhile, even in the midst of trials, she searches for her Beloved. She is struck and wounded by the watchmen of the city. -Song of Songs 5:7 Yet even in his absence, and even when her love is put to the test she is unmoved. She is totally preoccupied with Him. This is the "divine romance".

Finally, at the end of Solomon's Song those watching are amazed and ask,

"Who is this who comes up out of the wilderness, leaning upon her Beloved?" -Song of Solomon 8:5

God created man and women to have a free will. He will never try to re-engineer humans into automatons, androids or robots. And consent is always necessary in coming into covenant with God. A bride is always called to witness her marriage covenant. In this ceremony she will attest before other witnesses that she loves her betrothed. She will joyfully affirm that she has fully committed herself to Him. She testifies before a crowd of witnesses that she will follow Him if need be to the point of death. As Rebecca, in her part of the covenant ceremony she is pointedly asked,

"Will you go with this man?" -Gen.24:5

In her answer to God, to the watching host of angels, and to men she declares,
"I will".

By this witness she joins herself to him in the covenant of marriage.
And among those who watch and witness this betrothal ceremony of total commitment there are tears.
And the handkerchiefs come out.
But they are tears of joy.

THE COMMUNION CUP. HAVE WE DRUNK 'ALL OF IT'?

Is our relationship with Christ a one way street?

The communion cup involves a deeper commitment than that.

"And He took the cup and gave thanks, and gave it to them saying,
'Drink ye all of it.
For this is my blood of the new testament, which is shed for many, for the remission of sins." -Mat.26:27-28

Have we drunk *all* of it?
Do we know what "all" means?

LOVE AND GRACE ARE THE WELLSPRING OF THE END-TIME WITNESS.
THEY FULFILL AND TRANSCEND THE LEGAL REQUIREMENTS OF THE LAW.

Dear saints, this is not a matter of law. Our salvation is assured by our faith in Christ. It is covered by the blood sacrifice He made for us at the cross. But our love walk takes us beyond the realm of the law. Now we witness and walk out the covenant by His divine enabling grace, through faith. -Eph 2:8. We are carried across a threshold in a transport of Grace. And in that passage we enter into another dimension in God.

Our Christian faith runs quite a bit deeper than we have been told. As blood covenant Christians we are not passive observers. We are the Body and Bride of Christ. As we have shown, our witness for (or against) Jesus Christ, is inescapable. God is not just an impersonal Jedi "force" that we play around with. That road leads to witchcraft. Nor is God just a circular yin and yang of positive and negative energies that we try to "balance" in a humanistic way as eastern mysticism would have it. Life on this earth is more than just endless cycles of summer and winter, conquest and declension, sex and death. Holy history is laid out in a teleological linear fashion by the sovereign hand of God. He wrote the play of the ages. The story has its beginning and ending, its protagonists and its antagonists. The epic saga of life on this planet has a plot. There is an epic contest going on. This leads on into a climactic resolution in the closing scenes of the play.

God does not play dice with His universe. Nor is He an indifferent clockwork maker who has left the scene. YHVH-God, the God of Israel, has manifest Himself into this cosmos in Jesus Christ. Our "manifest destiny" is not bound up in this earth below but rather expressed in a blood covenant witness to **Him,** the One who came to earth from above! He is the Alpha and the Omega, the beginning and the end of all things. It is not what we know but WHO we know. This age of the gospel is the time of **His witness**. God's covenant people have been given a Great Commission, a quest and a glorious destiny. And they **will** be there when this age comes to its climactic end, when all is said and done.

FIRST COMING: THE SUFFERING SERVANT.
SECOND COMING: THE CONQUERING KING.
ARE WE READY FOR HIS RETURN?

2,000 years ago our Lord Jesus came to us as the Suffering Servant. He came as the Bridegroom to the bride, bringing His dowry, His gift, His offer of redemption. This next time it will be quite different. He will be returning as the conquering king. Yes, the long awaited Messiah will return to this earth. Jesus Christ/Yeshua Hamashiach will bring closure to the holy history of this age. The 7th seal will follow bringing in the final establishment of His glorious Millennial Kingdom.

THE COMMUNION CUP.
AND OUR PASSAGE BEYOND.

So the Communion Cup is a deeper matter than we had thought.
As we drink the Cup of Christ we pass through a threshold.
His Agape Love is wrapped around us.
In a divine serendipity we discover that,
"**......the love of God is shed abroad in our hearts by the Holy Spirit who has been given to us.**" -Rom.5:5

Suddenly we are beyond our self life.
We are "in Christ".

We are in the "communion of saints". -1Cor.10:16

Now, our desire, - our passion,
is to live out and to witness,
the covenant we co-signed with Him;
- even, if it comes down to that ultimate witness;
- the witness of our own blood.

This is the full implication of the blood covenant we have in Christ.
It is still an unpreached and untold story in the west.

This is the "rest of the story".

This is the full communion.

Q. So will the western church be called on again to witness the blood covenant of our Lord Jesus Christ?

A. In the first three centuries of church history we did.
And in countries abroad many Christian believers are bearing

faithful witness to the new covenant right at this very minute.

More people are being saved now than at any time in history.

And every day 500 Christians give their lives as witness/martyrs.

Q. How are they able to do this?

A. They are doing this by God's divine enabling grace.

Q. And why are they doing this?

A. They do this because of Love.

THE FLIGHT TO MYSTERY BOZRAH

Micah 2:12-13
& Revelation 12

An essay by Gavin Finley MD
endtimepilgrim.org - Aug. 2006

THE FLIGHT TO MYSTERY BOZRAH
AND THE BOZRAH EXILE

The Apostle John in the Book of Revelation tells us that in the latter days God's covenant people, the woman of Revelation 12, will be **given the wings of a great eagle** and she will fly off to a place of exile for three and a half years.

Here is our scripture passage.

REVELATION 12

1. Now a great sign appeared in heaven:
a woman clothed with the sun,
with the moon under her feet,
and on her head a garland of twelve stars.

2. Then being with child, she cried out in labor
and in pain to give birth.

3. And another sign appeared in heaven:
behold, a great, fiery red dragon
having seven heads and ten horns,
and seven diadems on his heads.

4. His tail drew a third of the stars of heaven and threw them to the earth. And the dragon stood before the woman who was ready to give birth, to devour her Child as soon as it was born.

5. She bore a male Child
who was to rule all nations with a rod of iron.
And her Child was caught up to God and His throne.

Now we come to the two scripture verses which form the crux of this article. It concerns the flight of the woman and the time period in which she is fed or nurtured. She will almost certainly be flying off to some remote place. It must be well separated and isolated from the main flows of international politics. In this place this woman of mystery is "fed" or "nurtured". We must assume this is nurturing in a spiritual as well as a physical sense.

6. Then the woman fled into the wilderness, where she has **a place prepared by God,** that they should **feed** her there **one thousand two hundred and sixty days.**

The very same message is restated 8 verses later. But this time the Holy Spirit gives it to us in terms of different time units:

14. But the woman was given **two wings of a great eagle,** that she might **fly into the wilderness to her place,** where

she is **nourished for a time and times and half a time,**
from the presence of the serpent.

15. So the serpent spewed water out of his mouth like a flood after the woman, that he might cause her to be carried away by the flood.
16. But the earth helped the woman, and the earth opened its mouth
and swallowed up the flood which the dragon had spewed out of his mouth.
17. And the dragon was enraged with the woman,
and he went to make war with the rest of her offspring,
who keep the commandments of God and have the testimony of Jesus Christ.

So here we have the great end time drama.
An epic persecution is being instigated by Satan.
'The woman' we see showcased throughout Holy Scripture,

Are the covenant people of the God of Israel.
They are entering into the Great Tribulation.

But wonder of wonders! What do we see?
The Woman is given the wings of a great eagle.
And she is flying away to "her place".
Where is she going?
And just what is going on here?

THE END-TIME GATHERING OF 'JACOB', "AS THE SHEEP OF BOZRAH" (WHICH IS A REFERENCE TO THE COVENANT PEOPLE OF GOD).

As usual, the Holy Scripture provides the best commentary.

The prophet Micah in Mic. 2:12-13 sheds some light on some of 'the rest of the story'.
Micah 2 King James Version
12. I will surely assemble, O **Jacob,** all of thee;
I will surely gather the **remnant of Israel;**
I will put them together **as the sheep of Bozrah,**
As the flock in the midst of their fold:
they shall make great noise
by reason of the multitude of men.

GOD WILL GATHER THE REMNANT OF ISRAEL. THE END-TIME REMNANT NATION OF ISRAEL, AND THE END-TIME REMNANT CONGREGATION OF ISRAEL WHICH IS THE END-TIME REMNANT CHURCH!

Here in Micah 2:12 we see an epic gathering of God's covenant people. The reference given here in the Old Testament is 'Jacob'. Micah refers to them as the 'remnant of Israel'. This reference to a 'remnant' clearly relates to God's covenant people after the refining. From other scripture we know that this refining occurs at the end of the age. Does it relate to the travail of the woman of destiny? The prophet Isaiah brings us this message.
Isaiah 48:10
"Behold I have refined thee, but not with silver;
I have **chosen** thee in the furnace of affliction."

The word "remnant" is a very helpful key here. It relates to God's Elect at the end of the age. A quick word search through the scriptures will soon make this clear. A remnant shall return" Isaiah says. (Isa.10:21, & 22) In

Micah 5 we see God has given His people Israel up; that is **until** an event of great significance. What is it? And does it relate to the flight of the woman we see in Revelation 12? It most definitely does.

WHAT HAPPENS WHEN THE REMNANT OF ISRAEL COME TO THE END OF THEIR STRENGTH?
WHAT HAPPENS WHEN THEY CAN NO LONGER "CARRY ON"?
OUR FATHER ABRAHAM FACED THIS TRIAL RIGHT AT THE VERY BEGINNING.

REMEMBER WHAT HAPPENED WHEN HE MADE COVENANT WITH Y'HOVAH-GOD?
GOD HIMSELF WILL BE CARRYING HIS PEOPLE IN THAT DAY.
THOSE ARE *HIS* FOOTPRINTS IN THE SAND; EVEN FOOTPRINTS THROUGH THE BLOOD.

We serve a God who loves His covenant people. He has never abandoned nor forsaken them. The sins of the prodigals may have carried them far away. But even in their wanderings they have always been close to the Father's heart. At the very beginning, even as the children of Israel were about to become a nation God carried them. He bore them **'on wings of eagles'** across the Red Sea in a great deliverance.

God declares His faithfulness in bearing and carrying His covenant people. As He carried them from their conception He will continue to do this until the nation is old. He will carry them right through to the consummation at the end of the age. This is a wonderful promise that will involve untold hundreds of millions of Y'hovah's **faithful Elect** in the latter days.

Isaiah 46:3-4 (GWF paraphrase)
3 Listen to me, O House of Jacob,
And all the remnant of the House of Israel,
Who have been carried by me from the belly,
Whom I carried from the womb.

4 Until you grow old I AM the One.
And until you turn gray I will carry you.
I have done this from your beginning,
and I will continue to bear you until the end;
I will rescue you, and carry you to safety.

THE TRAVAIL OF THE WOMAN
A REMNANT SHALL RETURN.
AND ALL ISRAEL WILL BE RESTORED

Here below in this Old Testament scripture we see the same woman of Israel John saw in Revelation 12. A great drama precedes the return of the remnant. This is a time of great travail. It is the Great Tribulation. Moses spoke of this tribulation. See this article.
And Jesus Himself prophesied that His covenant people would reject Him and would enter into a covenant with a false messiah. (John 5:43)
He also spoke of a time of travail and great tribulation. We see this laid out very clearly in Matthew 24, the Olivet Discouse.

The travail of 'the woman' was seen by John.
The prophet Micah also speaks of a great travail.

Micah 5:3 gives specific mention of the 'travail' of the woman.

Micah 5:3
"Therefore He will give them up,
until the time that **she which travaileth** hath brought forth.

Then the **remnant** of His brethren **shall return** unto the children of Israel."

This the travail clearly must precede and lead on to the deliverance and the glorification of the Man Child.
The travail of God's covenant people we see in the 5th seal is not in vain. It leads on to the 6th seal and the return of Messiah. This results in the end time restoration of all of Israel. Micah also tells of the glorious return of the remnant at the climax of the age.

In this same passage Micah tells the story of the casting away of Israel.
He also saw the travail of 'the woman' of Israel in the latter days.
Then he saw the climactic deliverance of the woman as the Man-child is born.
With this final magnificent restoration of all Israel a remnant returns.

Micah 5:3
"Therefore **He will give them up,**
until the time that she which travaileth hath brought forth. Then the **remnant** of His brethren **shall return** unto the children of Israel."

So it will be **a remnant** that will return. (Isa. 10:21-22)
This is God dealing with the Congregation of 'Israel'.

God will regather all His people.
There will come a great refinement involving all of Jacob/Israel with the wider Congregation/Church of God.
And **a remnant will return** at the end of the age.
What a magnificent story this is!

I WILL GATHER ALL OF YOU, O JACOB!

Our next big clue is in Micah 2:12.
God says He will gather 'all' of 'Jacob'.
God makes a big point of saying He will gather **'all'** of Jacob.

What is the Holy Spirit telling us here?

Jacob is a name for God's called out people. The Bible uses 'Jacob' in devotional and prophetic sense. This name is a handle for God's Covenant Congregation in their unrefined condition. In Bible symbology "Jacob" is the name they go by in their early pilgrimage. But at the end of their sojournings the company of 'Jacob'(trickster, supplanter, heel), has truly become "Israel", (prince with God).

THE WOMAN OF REVELATION 12.
A PICTURE OF THE COVENANT PEOPLE OF GOD

How might 'the woman' of Revelation 12 be pictured elsewhere in scripture?
We have seen connection to 'Jacob'.
'Jacob' is a name or 'handle' for the covenant people of God.

How about 'the woman'?
Is 'the woman' another Bible name for the covenant

people of God?
It certainly is!

In Genesis 3:15 we see reference to 'the woman' as the bearer of the Seed. The Seed of 'the woman' is the coming Messiah. And it is the Seed of the woman who will crush the head of the Serpent.

The Seed of the woman is certainly Jesus Christ, the Head.
Jesus Christ is also the Seed of Abraham.
The Seed of the Woman, the Seed of Abraham, relates to Christ our Head.
Does the Seed of the Woman, Seed of Abraham, have anything to do with us in the Body of Christ?
It certainly does. Our Apostle Paul tells us,

Galatians 3:29
"If you are **in Christ** then you too are **Abraham's Seed** and heirs according to the promise (given to Abraham)."

"The promise" refers to the promise of the Land of Israel. It also refers to the promise of a myriad company of descendents,
a huge multitude, a "melo-hagoyim" that cannot be counted for numbers.

So here in Revelation 12 we see the Woman, her Seed, and the dragon once again. The drama between the woman and the serpent we saw back in the Garden of Eden. It has now come full circle. 'The woman' of destiny is now in the end time. She is in travail and in great tribulation.

The Woman of wonder we see in Revelation 12 must be restored Israel. Because she has a diadem, a crown of 12 stars. When John saw her she was in great travail. And yet she is dazzling, clothed with the sun in the brightness of her Heavenly Father. The moon and her own reflected light are no longer dominant. The moon is beneath her feet.

In the Song of Songs we get another glimpse of this woman of great wonder. It is the grand conclusion of the story and the end of the song. The daughters of Jerusalem, in all their worldliness, can only gaze on her with wonder. They ask,

SONG OF SONGS 6
10. "Who is she who arises as the dawn, from the womb of the morning,
fair and beautiful as the moon,
clear and bright, dazzling as the sun,
as awesome and as terrible as an army with banners!?"

THE REFERENCES TO 'BOZRAH' AT THE END OF THE AGE.
STILL AN UNTOLD STORY.

It is in this end time context that we see the flight of the woman of Revelation 12.
She is obviously flying off to a place of mystery that has some prominence in the end time.
Is there a place mentioned elsewhere in Holy Scripture that may provide a cross reference?
Indeed there is.
It is a place the Bible identifies as 'Bozrah'.

We know from the context of the Bozrah scriptures in Micah and in Isaiah 63 that Bozrah is a place of exile for God's people in the latter days. It is also a place of an

awesome climactic deliverance at the end of the age.
Because Messiah returns in wrath to Bozrah. He is coming to destroy the wicked. And he is returning to break out His people from some sort of enclosure at Bozrah. It will be at Bozrah that Messiah will come to rescue His saints, described as the sheep of Bozrah, at the magnificent 'Bozrah Deliverance'. Here is our scripture from Mic. 12:12-13.

Micah 2 King James Version
12. I will surely assemble, O Jacob, all of thee;
I will surely gather the remnant of Israel;
I will put them together as the sheep of Bozrah,
As the flock in the midst of their fold:
they shall make great noise
by reason of the multitude of men.

Here in Micah 2:12 God's people 'Jacob' are being gathered.
They are being gathered at a place called 'Bozrah'.
And from the other Bozrah scripture in Isaiah 63 there can be no doubt.
The Bozrah scriptures relate to the end time.
God's covenant people have taken flight.
And they have landed at a place referred to in scripture as 'Bozrah'.

So much for the gathering.
What happens at the **end** of the Bozrah story?

The answer is awesome beyond words to tell.
We see Messiah coming to His fold in the early dawn.
He is a fearsome Presence as He strides in.
As the Shepherd of Israel He is right in among His people.
He comes to make a Way through the wall of the

sheepfold.
His sheep are pressing in around Him with great pressure. But He is 'The Breaker'. And as the dawn breaks the breakthrough comes.
The Shepherd of Israel becomes the Door of the sheepfold. And then He is leading His sheep out to pasture.

13. The Breaker is come up before them:
they have broken up,
and have passed through the gate,
and are gone out by it:
and their king shall pass before them,
and the LORD on the head of them.
- Mic. 2:12-13 KJV

God expects us to study the Holy Scriptures and connect the dots. (2Tim.2:15 & 3:16) The deliverance of the remnant of God's people out at Bozrah presupposes an exile in Bozrah. And the Revelation 12 scripture prophesies a flight to a place of safety for God's people at the end of the age. So are Revelation 12 and the flight and exile of the woman and the gathering of God's people at Bozrah connected? I believe that we are bound to say that they are connected. They are two perspectives of the same end time story. God is taking care of His covenant people right up there at the end of the age.

So here our Apostle John is bringing us "the rest of the story". Here we have a wonderful promise showing God's great mercy and deliverance. The flight of the woman of Revelation 12 completes the story of the end time exile at Bozrah. Because Bozrah is surely the destination of the woman of destiny in this epic saga prophesied for the end of this age.

THE FLIGHT OF THE WOMAN OF REVELATION 12. AND THE TIME PERIOD COINCIDES WITH THE GREAT TRIBULATION PERIOD.

The scripture passage in Revelation 12 is stark and plain. God's covenant people will fly off to a place of safety, feeding, or nurturing, in the latter days. We are clearly and concisely told that they will be sheltered and fed, (or nurtured), during a certain time period. That time period happens to be the very same time period of the Great Tribulation. (Dan.12:7) It coincides exactly with the reign of the Antichrist. (Rev.13:5). It is also the precise time period John gives for the trampling of Jerusalem. (Rev.11:2) This is the latter half of the 70th Week of Daniel. We are talking here about the final three and a half years of this age. Here are the details.

The time period during which the woman is nurtured is given in two ways. In Revelation 12:6 we are told that the covenant people of God are fed or nurtured for 1260 days. In Revelation 12:14 we get the very same information. But here in this verse the message is restated in terms of different time units. The time period for the exile of the woman is given in verse 14 as a "time, times, and half a time", or a period of three and a half **Biblical years**.

The flight and exile of the woman is a scriptural bonanza. It gives us a veritable "Rosetta stone" for prophetic time. Because the Ancient of Days dispenses it to us from the courts of heaven in two separate ways. The time is dispensed to us in **two** time units, those being **days** and **biblical years**. This is a clincher for Bible prophecy students. A Biblical year is **360 days**, period! There is no question about it.

Here is our math. 1260 divided by 3.5 = 360. So the number of days in a biblical or prophetic year is 360 days. This is in harmony with the Biblical time or holy time we see dispensed to us throughout the Holy Scriptures.

The flight and exile of the woman John has given to us in these two verses tells us something else as well. The flight and exile of the woman is also the time period of the latter half of the 70th Week of Daniel.

God's covenant people in the end-time drama are showcased in scripture in several ways.
Moses prophesied that God's people would eventually get themselves into some serious trouble.
He specifically stated that they would be in tribulation in the latter days.
Jesus described His people as 'the Elect'.
And He told of a Great Tribulation in the Olivet Discourse.
We also see God's covenant people pictured as 'the woman' in Revelation 12.
They the people of faith, the Congregation of Abraham, Isaac, and Jacob.
They are called 'Jacob' in Micah 2:12-13.
Here in Micah we see them gathered in exile. Micah identifies and characterizes them here "as the sheep of Bozrah". (Mic. 12:12-13)
Why are God's remnant Elect being gathered together by God in a place of exile?
What is going on here? And why did this happen?

The Apostle John does not tell us the reason the woman is compromised and in this great danger. But other scriptures do. It seems that here will be a "great falling away" from the faith or an 'apostasy' at the end of this age.

(2Thes.2:3) It will involve the 7 year covenant of Daniel 9:27, probably the most important prophetic scripture of all. Jesus Himself said that He came in His Father's Name. But His covenant people would reject Him and choose someone else who came in **his own name**, a Luciferian selfist, a false messiah. (John 5:43)

But John does give us valuable information. He tells us that the woman is taking flight to a place where she can be cared for. It is quite obviously a place of exile. He certainly does gives us some valuable details concerning that flight and that exile. He tells us that the woman is threatened by the Dragon, Satan or Lucifer. She is also in travail and about to complete the delivery of a man child. This is why she has to flee to a place of exile.

The 'woman' is given the wings of a great eagle. Apparently during the end time drama the covenant people of God will be given the means to flee to a place of safety. (Rev.12:6) This is almost certainly an airlift of epic, even biblical proportions. And the mention of a **'great eagle'** gives us a clue as to which nation will be providing the airlift. There in that place of exile they will be protected and spiritually fed or **nourished**. (Rev.12:6 & 12:14) This exile lasts for a period of three and a half biblical years or 1260 days. (Rev.12:6 & 12:14) This is the very same time period of the Great Tribulation or **'Jacob's trouble'**.

GOMER'S FINAL DALLIANCE LEADS TO "JACOB'S TROUBLE". COMPROMISE WITH THE WORLD CAUSES GOD'S COVENANT PEOPLE TO ENTER INTO THE GREAT TRIBULATION.

Jeremiah 30
7. "Alas, for that day is great, so that none is like it.
And it is the time of **Jacob's trouble,**
But he shall be saved out of it.

'Jacob's trouble' is the Great Tribulation. (Dan.12:6-7)
It is the time period of the reign of the Antichrist. (Rev.13:5)
And it is the exact same time period of the trampling of Jerusalem. (Rev.11:2)

How did God's people get into this jam?
Apparently 'the woman' is as Gomer.
Moses gave a warning to God's people about this. (Deut. 4:23-31)
Moses prophesied in his final address to the covenant people of God that this End-Time Apostasy would happen.
So did Jesus in **John 5:43**
God's people have had a continuing pattern of aberrant behavior. In departing from their First Love and True Husband they seek protection and solace from their angst by taking worldly lovers.
Here we see 'the woman', (Israel and the Church), in her final dalliance.
It will be her final and cataclysmic mistake.
She has made covenant with a false messiah.
Now she is in a world of trouble.

But, all is not lost.
Something else of great wonder is happening.
And it is happening right inside the Tribulation period.
A great drama is unfolding during last half of the last seven years of this age.
The woman is being threatened by the dragon who is empowering the Antichrist.

She is also in travail and in pain to be delivered.
But nevertheless, this is a magnificent prophecy.
Because the woman is wearing the starry crown.

Let us pause to take in the big picture here.
The **Head** of the Manchild is most certainly our Lord Jesus Christ.
He is our sacred Head. And He has already been born.
He has already been resurrected to glory.
Jesus was the firstfruits from the dead. (1Cor. 15:20)
He rose from the dead and ascended to His Father nearly 2,000 years ago.
But there is more to this travail and delivery of the Manchild than we have been told.

The **Body** of the Manchild and the entire Body of Christ is in the story as well.
The Elect, the Body of Christ, will be born into the glory as well.
The Manchild is sacrificed in the drama of the 5th seal. (Rev.6:9-11)
Here the 'final witness' of the saints is brought before the courts of heaven.
And then their souls are seen in glory, even as the ashes beneath the altar in heaven.
John sees this great company gathering before the throne of God. (Rev. 12:5)
And God the Father, the Ancient of Days, is about to give the word to wrap things up. (Rev. 16:1)

When that 5th seal final witness of the saints is complete the 6th seal follows. (Rev.6:12-13)
The heavens open and the sign of the Son of Man is seen in heaven. (Mat.24:30)

The great harvest of the end time is about to be reaped. (Rev.14:14-20)

Meanwhile, the woman of Revelation 12 is in great travail as she is being delivered. (Rev.12:1-2)
She has been given the wings of a **great eagle**.
Can we guess which nation might be involved here?
She flees into the wilderness away from the face of the dragon. (Rev.12:6)
God, once again, is showing His great mercy in deliverance. And a certain country is aiding her in her flight away from the face of the Dragon.
She is on her way. She is on her flight to a place of exile.

That place of gathering and exile is identified in Micah 2:12-13 with the name 'Bozrah'.
Bozrah means 'sheepfold'. And this is our first major clue.
In former times Bozrah was a pastoral city of Edom.
It belonged to the children of **Esau** .
And that is our other clue.

THE PLACE OF THE EXILE IS GIVEN IN MICAH 2:12-13 AS BOZRAH. IT IS NOT PETRA. PETRA WOULD NOT ACCOMODATE MORE THAN 1,000 PEOPLE. THE END-TIME EXILE OF JACOB, GOD'S COVENANT PEOPLE, INVOLVES HUNDREDS OF MILLIONS OF SAINTS. FOR THOSE FLEEING JERUSALEM A REFUGE AT PETRA WOULD BE AN UNWISE AND A FATAL CHOICE. THE WHOLE MIDDLE EAST WILL BE A WAR ZONE! GAS WARFARE OR FUEL BOMBS WOULD QUICKLY

TURN THE DEEP CANYONS OF PETRA INTO A DEATH TRAP.

The name of the place of exile to which 'the woman' flees is given to us in scripture. It is **Bozrah**. And it is right there in Mystery Bozrah that Messiah, (and Micah refers to Him as "the Breaker"), will come to destroy the wicked and deliver His saints at the end of the age. The place of refuge will not be Petra. There are **no** scripture passages that mention Petra or allude in any way to Petra at all. None, zero, zip.

Why have our Bible prophecy teachers done this switch from Biblical Bozrah to un-Biblical Petra? Why hide the solid Bozrah scriptures with a false and misleading fable about Petra? Will the saints of the **Commonwealth of Israel**, particularly women and children, really find shelter right inside the End-Time drama and right in the middle of an apocalyptic war zone that will encompass the entire Middle East? Can the hundreds of millions of saints in Greater Israel really expect to crowd into this small little waterless canyon and find refuge and expect to survive there throughout the entire 3.5 years of the Great Tribulation?

Here are the facts that hopefully will put this sham, this cover story to rest. Petra has **never** been able to house and accommodate more than 1,000 people. There is no water there and no sewage, - just empty caves and tombs of hard rock. Clearly Petra is not big enough to house and shelter nor supply food and other supplies for the huge numbers of people God will be sheltering in the latter days. And certainly not for three and a half years in a war zone with no good roads, no railway, and no airfields. Getting supplies into Petra under these circumstances would be difficult.

Petra is an unlikely, even impossible place, for an exile of the nation of Israel or even the small 5 million population from Judah and Jerusalem. The place is too small. And Petra certainly wouldn't accommodate a wider company of Christian and Messianic believers in an exile that numbers in the hundreds of millions. And if we are considering a refuge for Israel during the Armageddon siege then we need to be brought up to date. Yes, in ancient times Petra was a retreat for the Idumeans. The narrow passes were easily defended with swords and bows and arrows. But in these days of modern warfare the Israeli military would never allow their women and children to be led to an unsafe place like Petra in Jordan. In this day and age there is no shelter there. They would be far better off staying at home back in Israel in their underground bomb shelters. Petra would **never** qualify as a retreat in this day and age, except in the fevered imaginations of Bible prophecy story tellers and their unthinking audiences. Even getting a population of people out to Petra would expose them to great dangers on the way. Then to put a population of civilians in Petra at a dangerous location right inside a war zone would be sheer madness. It would seal their doom. Petra would be a deathtrap.

And why? Because one bomb down in that deep gorge would be the end of all the people in there. And with a chemical bomb the gas would just sit in the gorge and go nowhere. A gas attack would kill the whole population in that valley very quickly. And in the modern era of napalm bombs and fuel bombs a retreat to Petra would be utterly suicidal. The gorge would soon become a fiery furnace. The supposed "place of refuge" would soon become an oven full of charred corpses. No one would survive.

So what is going on here? Why was the Bozrah story we see clearly outlined in Isaiah 63 and Micah 2:12-13 being dumped? Why is the true and faithful **Bozrah exile** being "cloaked" by this hare-brained unscriptural and fanciful "flight to Petra" story? Why was this Petra fable floated anyway? Prophecy teachers talk a lot about Petra. But virtually nothing is being taught about Bozrah. Why the misinformation? And what is the real agenda here?

That, dear saints, is what we shall be looking into in this article.

BOZRAH, NOT PETRA.
THE REAL STORY IS THE FLIGHT OF THE WOMAN, GOD'S ELECT, TO A PLACE OF EXILE AND NURTURING DURING THE TRIBULATION. THE BIBLE CALLS IT BOZRAH AND IT IS PROBABLY A FARAWAY PLACE. THAT STORY IS BEING SWITCHED OUT IN EXCHANGE FOR A FALSE STORY ABOUT A SUPPOSED ESCAPE TO PETRA BY THE POPULATION OF ISRAEL.

The Bozrah story tells of a magnificent deliverance of God's people at the end of the age. It involves the returning Messiah and the covenant people of the God of Abraham, Isaac, and Jacob. The scriptures point to Bozrah as a place where the Elect are held in exile during the time of "Jacob's trouble". They are held captive under the jurisdiction of the wild, untamed, and Godless children of Esau.

Here is something we need to understand. The prophecy of Isaac over his son Esau way back in Genesis still stands. The Edomites are still with us today. An epic future time, the 70th Week of Daniel, will see them rise up just as Isaac prophesied. (Gen.27:39-40) The wild and godless Edomites will eventually be given dominion over God's covenant people.

Micah sees end time exile and incarceration of God's covenant people in the end time drama. He also sees the second coming of Messiah and the epic conclusion to the Bozrah story. He sees the Shepherd of Israel entering His sheepfold in the hours before dawn. Out there at Bozrah our returning Messiah becomes "the Breaker".

This wonderful prophecy of the Bozrah Deliverance is hidden from Christian eyes at this point in history. It is "cloaked" by the powers that be. A Bozrah deliverance presupposes a Bozrah exile. We are looking here at an incarceration of God's covenant people in the last 3.5 years of the age. This may be cross-referenced by John the Beloved as the flight of the woman of Revelation 12.

This is very disturbing to some Christian believers. The rulers are well aware of past Church history. They probably fear that this information, (should it get out), may trigger societal disruptions by carnal Christians. And so at this point in time the entire Bozrah drama is under a religious smokescreen involving a supposed flight of Israel to a place of refuge in Petra. The flight to Bozrah is still an untold story.

Here below is the scripture in Micah that tells of the Bozrah deliverance. This scripture is in the Old Testament. We are not used to looking for the second coming in the Old Testament. So the prophetic significance of the Bozrah scriptures are missed by dispensational Bible teachers in the Church. Bozrah is rarely mentioned by today's teachers of Bible prophecy. And yet here it is.

Micah 2
Hebrew Names Version of World English Bible

12. I will surely assemble, Ya`akov, all of you;
I will surely gather the remnant of Yisra'el;
I will put them together as the sheep of Botzrah,
As a flock in the midst of their pasture;
They will throng with people.

13. He who breaks open the way goes up before them.
They break through the gate, and go out.
And their king passes on before them,
With the LORD at their head."

Micah 2
King James Version

12. I will surely assemble, O Jacob, all of thee;
I will surely gather the remnant of Israel;
I will put them together as the sheep of Bozrah,
As the flock in the midst of their fold:

they shall make great noise
by reason of the multitude of men.

13. The breaker is come up before them:
they have broken up,
and have passed through the gate,
and are gone out by it:
and their king shall pass before them,
and the LORD on the head of them.
-Mic. 2:12-13 KJV

The image above shows a stone sheepfold of the type seen in biblical times. Here the sheep would be confined by their shepherd during the hours of darkness in a place of protection. As the dawn approached the shepherd would come into the sheepfold among His sheep. They would gather around the shepherd as he prepared to open a way for them to be delivered from the stone enclosure. As he opened a way out for them they would crowd up alongside him pushing against the gateway with a lot of force.

When the breakthrough came the whole flock would pour out of the sheepfold through the breach together with the Messiah as "the Breaker" going before them. They would follow on the heels of the Shepherd as he led them out to find pasture. This is the magnificent pastoral picture of the "manchild company" breaking forth into holy history at the end of the age. This will change the destiny of heaven and earth. The stars and angelic rulerships fall. And here on earth Messiah brings in His Millennial Kingdom. He will minister and rule for a thousand years.

This detailed picture of the deliverance of the elect **by Messiah** (and not the church) at the Second Advent is given to us in Micah chapter 2. This drama is laid out for us quite clearly and in detail.

The Bozrah deliverance is a thrilling element of the Second Coming of Christ. He is the Anointed One and our coming Messiah. The Micah 2 scripture shows the connection of the Second Coming of Christ to Bozrah, (an Edomite domain), very well. We also see The Bozrah deliverance laid out for us in spectacular fashion in **Isaiah 63.** This is the judgment side to the Second Coming of Christ. God is obviously telling us something here in these Bozrah scriptures. Each of them clearly relate to the return of Messiah.

BOZRAH, NOT PETRA.
THE "FLIGHT TO PETRA" IS BASED ON HUMAN SPECULATION.
THERE ARE NO REFERENCES TO PETRA IN THE BIBLE.
BUT THERE ARE MANY BOZRAH SCRIPTURES.

If evangelicals are going to present a story of a flight to Petra in the time of the Great Tribulation then where are the scriptures supporting such a notion?
Are there **any** verses at all in the Bible that mention Petra at all?
The short answer is this.

There are none! No, not one!

THE SPLITTING OF THE MOUNT OF OLIVES AT THE SECOND COMING,
AND THE FLIGHT OF THE INHABITANTS OF JERUSALEM TO AZAL

Evangelical teachers seem to ignore or put a news blackout on this wonderful story of the flight to Bozrah. And we hear nothing from them concerning the magnificent Bozrah deliverance at the end of this age. It seems that they do a bait and switch. The Bozrah prophecy is obfuscated and "cloaked". Instead we get an unsubstantiated substitute story about a supposed flight to Petra in the time of Armageddon and the second coming. They have a notion that Petra, an ancient city in Jordan would be a nice place of refuge for refugees coming out of Jerusalem during the big earthquake that splits the Mount of Olives at the end of this age. But is there any scripture at all to support this notion?

The answer is "no".

Well there will certainly be an epic earthquake at the end of this age. Zechariah tells us that it will split the Mount of Olives in half. And the inhabitants of Jerusalem will flee. But where will they flee to?
Are they really going to Petra?
And if not, then just where will they flee?

This "flight to Petra" notion is embedded in the evangelical family. Biblical Christians bring it up quite often. It is brought up in relation to the trials of the Jewish people in Jerusalem and their flight out of the city of Jerusalem at the end of the age. But where did this idea of a "flight to Petra" way down in Jordan come from?

As we shall see, it is an unscriptural fable thought up by men.
There is no scriptural support for a "flight to Petra" at all.

The scripture passage they focus in on to support this is in Zechariah 14.
But as we shall see, they have the wrong city.

ZECHARIAH 14
1 Behold, the day of the Lord is coming,
And your spoil will be divided in your midst.
2 For I will gather all the nations to battle against Jerusalem;
The city shall be taken,
The houses rifled,
And the women ravished.
Half of the city shall go into captivity,
But the remnant of the people shall not be cut off from the city.
3 Then the Lord will go forth And fight against those nations,
As He fights in the day of battle.
4 And in that day His feet will stand on the Mount of Olives,

Which faces Jerusalem on the east.
And the Mount of Olives shall be split in two,
From east to west,
Making a very large valley;
Half of the mountain shall move toward the north
And half of it toward the south.
5 Then you shall flee through My mountain valley,

For the mountain valley shall reach to AZAL.
Yes, you shall flee As you fled from the earthquake
In the days of Uzziah king of Judah.
Thus the Lord my God will come,
And all the saints with You.*

THE ESCAPE FROM THE EARTHQUAKE BY THE INHABITANTS OF JERUSALEM.
WHEN THE MOUNT OF OLIVES IS SPLIT THEY EVACUATE TO NEARBY AZAL.

As we can see, there is no mention of Bozrah or Petra at all in this passage.
This is a flight of the inhabitants of Jerusalem out of the city during an earthquake.
That earthquake is the "big one" and it splits the Mount of Olives.
One element of the Second Coming is Jesus' return at the Mount of Olives.
He is the One who at His Second Coming causes the earthquake!

In this prophecy all the prophecies involving Edom there is no mention at all of the city of Petra.
And there is no mention of Petra in any other part of the Bible for that matter.
But here **is** a clear message of a flight out of Jerusalem that will end up in a nearby city.
That city is not way down in Jordan. It is in fact quite close to Jerusalem.
It is the **city of Azal**.

This "flight to Azal" happens at the very end of the age at the second coming of Christ.
The "flight to Azal" we see in the passage above involves a short time short distance evacuation of a city.
Zechariah gives no mention of a prolonged Tribulation refuge way down in Petra which is in Jordan.
This "flight to Azal" will not satisfy the prophecy of the 'flight of the woman' in Rev. 12:6 & 12:14.
Nor will not satisfy the scripture of the Bozrah exile and the Bozrah deliverance we see in Micah 2:12-13.

The so called "flight to Petra" is a doctrine without any scriptural foundation whatsoever.
The 'Azal evacuation' scripture in Zechariah 14 is the real story.
And yet it and the Bozrah scriptures have both been used to build up this Petra fable.
This "flight to Petra" and "refuge in Petra" fable is religious folklore.
They are used in a fast and loose way to "cover up" the rue stories at Azal and at Bozrah.
The Petra retreat fable becomes a "cover story" for these real prophecies.
Because we know that there will be a citywide evacaution of Jerusalem to nearby Azal.
And we know that Messiah will be paying a visit to Bozrah at His Second Coming. (Isa. 63 and Micah 2:12-13)

A RELIGIOUS SMOKESCREEN OVER THE BOZRAH EXILE.
AND A "CLOAKING" OF THE BOZRAH DELIVERANCE.

Now we come to the next question. Why has this crucial information regarding the exile and subsequent deliverance of God's elect from Edomite incarceration at Bozrah at the end of the age been "cloaked"? Why have we been fed this Petra disinformation? What are the dark rulers pulling ecclesiastical strings. Just what are they trying to do here? Just what is their agenda? Why have the Bozrah scriptures in Micah 2:12-13 and the Revelation 12 scripture been omitted from teachings on end-time themes?

The Bozrah exile is a story of a retreat to a place of sanctuary during the great Tribulation is it not? And the following Bozrah deliverance one of the most exciting and inspiring passages in the Bible. The entire Bozrah drama has obviously been "cloaked" by the religious powers. Why? Isn't the Bozrah story some exceedingly good and encouraging news?
So why haven't we heard this before?

THE POLITICS OF END TIME TRUTH

Well it seems that when it comes to the question of the Great Tribulation Christian Bible teachers do not want to have to tell the Church they might be involved in any sort of exile. Even if it is outlined in the Bible in Micah 2:12-13 and in Revelation 12:6 and 12:14 they will studiously omit any reference to it as an end time scripture involving the Church. These dark dramas of the end-time, according to them, are are "not for the Church". They are "for the Jews".

Of course we know that this Great Tribulation, is the time of "Jacob's trouble". Therefore, according to them, the

Great Tribulation will be a time of trial and tribulation specifically for the Jews and the Jews only. But is this true? Is there any scriptural proof that the Church will not be here during the 70th Week?

Bible teachers know that the returning Messiah will deliver our Jewish brethren when He comes back and His feet touch the Mount of Olives. When Jesus returns He will deliver the Jewish nation from the end-time siege by the surrounding nations at Jerusalem. - Zech.12:7-13:1 Christians know all about the deliverance of Israel at the Battle of Armageddon. But is this all there is to the Second Coming of Christ? Is there more? Perhaps something they have not been told?

What Christians do **not** know is that at His Second Coming Christ will also come in vengeance upon His enemies at Bozrah. (Isa.63) He will also deliver His saints at the same place, (or places), named in scripture as **Bozrah.** Bozrah means "sheepfold". And it is a place under the end time sovereignty of Edom. These are two very valuable clues to the Bozrah story as it relates to the climax of this age.

Bozrah is part and parcel of the end time drama. The exile to sanctuary in Bozrah and these deliverance actions by Messiah at Bozrah have not been taught by Bible prophecy teachers. But they are all part of the mosaic of this magnificent return of Messiah. Because He is coming back! And He will deliver and then glorify all His covenant people both in Israel and out in the nations. All this drama and adventure will be capped off at the **Resurrection-Rapture** at the end of the age.

The "cloaking" of this information is probably done with good intentions. It has been hidden from the Church at large and it has been kept from them for their own good. The western Church is still immature. Even we as evangelicals are still a carnal and potentially violent people. So perhaps we did not deserve to know this Bozrah story.

But with this prophecy the faithful Elect are given hope. With a God who carries His people we don't *need* to fear. We don't *need* to be angry and violent crusading dominionists, beating our fellow servants. God has everything under control, even in the midst of Great Tribulation. According to Micah and the Apostle John our God will be merciful. He will nurture and feed His people **during** the Great Tribulation. He will take them a place of exile, a mystery place named in Holy Scripture as Bozrah.

Bozrah was a pastoral town in Edom. So we know it has some connection to the Edomites. And the modern day children of Jacob's godless brother Esau will be in control. But if God says that the woman of Revelation 12 will be **"nurtured"** then some positive things must be going on. This will be a camp-meeting of Biblical proportions. The remnant of all 12 tribes of Israel will be there. Micah says that *ALL* of Jacob will be gathered. (Micah 2:12-13). This will include a remnant of our Jewish brothers and sisters in the House of Judah. It will also have to include the remnant of the **lost 10 tribes**.

And here is some more encouraging news. Just as in that former seven year famine back in Egypt, there will be "a famine of the hearing of the Word of God". (Amos 8:11) During the seven years of the future 70th Week God's people will be hungry for spiritual truth. And once again the **House of Joseph** will be feeding his brethren and the world, just as our patriarch Joseph did in the former time in Egypt. The House of Joseph will be there, emerging from the shadows, along with the House of Benjamin. Once again Joseph will be laying out a table for his brethren. He will be revealing the mysteries, even in the midst of tears.

So is this Bozrah prophecy all bad? Just what will be happening during the Tribulation period out at the sheepfolds of Bozrah?

Quite clearly the Bozrah exile will not just be an incarceration story. Apparently the Bozrah enclosure also provide some degree of **shelter** and even **nurturing or spiritual nourishment** for the children of Abraham, Isaac, and Jacob in the end-time. Bozrah is in fact a place of relative safety.

THE FLIGHT TO BOZRAH AND THE GATHERING OF ALL OF JACOB IN MICAH 2:12-13.
AND THE FLIGHT OF THE WOMAN OF REVELATION 12:8 & 12:14.
THEY ARE ONE AND THE SAME.

To pick up the rest of the story we shall now go to the apocalypse of John. In the saga of 'the woman of Revelation 12' we see the story of the flight of the woman, (a picture of God's covenant people), "away from the face of the dragon". She is obviously taken off to a place of exile. And the **time** of this exile corresponds to the time of the latter half of the 70th Week of Daniel, the final 3.5 years of this age. This is the time of the Great Tribulation and the trampling of Jerusalem.

Why is the woman in exile for three and a half years?
As we study the scripture passage in Revelation 12 we see that she is there for two purposes.

1. She is there to be protected. And
2. She is there to be nurtured.

This must mean a spiritual nurturing or nourishment. She will be physically cared for too it seems. This prophecy of the woman who takes flight on the wings of an eagle to a place of nurturing for the exact time period of the Great Tribulation is clearly telling us a very important part of the story of the end-time. It parallels the story of the exile of the children of Abraham, Isaac, and Jacob in the end-time at Bozrah. Bozrah is the place, (or places), where Jacob can be nurtured in the things of God. This will be happening during the last half of the 70th week, and during the time of the Great Tribulation.

The Bozrah story cannot be hidden forever. It will be told eventually. Bozrah is an important spiritual place in which God will protect, preserve, refine, and nurture His people in the end-time drama.

Where will end-time Bozrah be located? Right now we do not know where Bozrah might be geographically. It may be many places. Or it may be one place. It may be one central dumping ground for Judeo-Christian troublemakers in the latter days.

Oh yes, the Bozrah scriptures do not just refer to "past history". Nor is Bozrah just an archeological dig on a ruin of an ancient pastoral city of Esau southeast of the Dead Sea. For those who are there at this appointed place and time in the latter days God will have His purpose for this exile. Bozrah will be the place the prophets Isaiah and Micah spoke about. Bozrah will be a very real place under the overall control of very real modern day Edomites. It may well turn out to be a geo-political area far from the Promised Land. Mystery Bozrah of the latter days will most certainly be a modern geo-political area. The poetic prophecy indicates that Mystery Bozrah will be out at **the ends of the earth**. The covenant people of God will look up in those days to find themselves in a serendipity. It will be the place of great wonder, of wrath and deliverance. It will be the place and time the Old Testament prophets spoke of over 2700 years ago. A place and time the patriarchs of old saw **in the stars and constellations** in the heavens.

And there, in that place, they will find their God.
They will find Him in a place that will be

" . . .as a hiding place from the wind;
A covert from the tempest,
Even a shelter in the time of storm.

As rivers of water in a dry and thirsty place,
As the shadow of a great Rock,
in a weary land." (Isa.32:2)

-o-o-o-o-o-o-o-o-o-o-o-o-o-o-o-o-o-o-o-o-o-o-o-o-o-o-o-o-o-o-o-o-o-

And that is where Messiah
Will find them at the end.

A day of wrath, deliverance;
"The Breaker" comes to rend,

He comes into His sheepfold;
They all press in to Him.
Then at the Door the breakthrough!
Out they go! Led by their King!

This is no fable. All of this will certainly happen.
In the **Fall Season** of some future year.
This end-time drama will unfold precisely as it has been written.
Messiah will surely return as "the Breaker".
At the sheepfolds of Mystery Bozrah. - Mic.2:12,&13

THE BOZRAH EXILE

Micah 2:12-13 & Rev. 12

An essay by Gavin Finley MD
endtimepilgrim.org - 2006

THE FLIGHT TO BOZRAH AND THE BOZRAH EXILE

The Apostle John in the Book of Revelation tells us that in the latter days God's covenant people, (in this passage characterized as the woman of Revelation 12), will be in a measure of travail or tribulation. (Moses' prophecy also concurs with this.) The woman will be **given the wings of a great eagle** and she will fly off to "her place", a wilderness place of exile for a period of three and a half years. (Rev. 12:14) Eight verses earlier in the same chapter the Apostle John is given the same period of time, the exile and nurturing of the woman, in terms of 1260 days. (Rev. 12:6) This gives us a 'Rosetta stone' of sorts for Biblical or prophetic time. This final 3.5 years, 42 months, or 1260 days of this age is measured out for us in very precise terms by the Holy Spirit in seven different Bible verses.

The Bozrah exile embodies a magnificent promise. God's covenant people, many of them mothers and children, will be given a partial reprieve from the Great Tribulation at the end of this age. They will be given the means to fly off to a place "away from the face of the dragon". This is a promise of God. We can be 100% sure that this coming great exodus and regathering of God's covenant people will happen.

The prophet Micah in Mic. 2:12-13 brings us 'the rest of the story'. He tells us where God's covenant people are fleeing to in this epic end time drama. God says He will gather all His covenant people at a secret mystery place the Bible identifies as 'Bozrah'.

Micah 2
Hebrew Names Version of World English Bible

12. I will surely assemble, Ya`akov, (Jacob), all of you;
I will surely gather the remnant of Yisra'el, (Israel);
I will put them together as the sheep of Botzrah,
As a flock in the midst of their pasture;
They will throng with people.

This is the epic end-time migration of people we might call the "Bozrah Exile". Bozrah was an ancient city, (now a ruin), belonging to the Edomites the godless children of Esau. This is an awesome prophecy, and one that few Bible teachers know about or feel free to speak about. And so this redemptive and inspiring story of that epic end-time retreat from the face of the Dragon arranged by God for His covenant people in the final 3.5 years of this age still remains untold.

So there at a mysterious place the Bible calls "Bozrah" the people Micah calls "Jacob" will gather. "Jacob" is a precursor spiritual state before God's covenant people become "Israel", prince with God. God through Micah says "I will gather **all of you**"! So this company of people, the Congregation/Church God loves will be huge, probably numbering in the hundreds of millions. We are talking here of people from all around the world regathered from all twelve tribes of Israel. This stupendous exile will include those who have been regathered and "called out" of the 'lost 10 tribes of Israel'. This is that Greater Israel spoken of by our Apostle Paul in Ephesians 2:12-13 as the 'Commonwealth of Israel'. They will be "called out" to become God's final "ekklesia", His Congregation/Church/Synagogue. **All** of them, and the bulk of them 666 rejecters, will be regathered.

We know that God's covenant people in their unrefined form as Jacob will be refined at last to become Israel. And yes, this will be a time of trial and a refining to be sure. But this is is not a grievous thing at all for those who are being called out and are responding to YHVH-God by grace through faith in His Holy Word. They will be spiritually preserved under the guidance and comfort of God's Holy Spirit. And there at Bozrah, in that mystery place yet unknown, all of God's covenant people will be sheltered, fed, and nurtured. Mystery Bozrah will be the place where a lot of Biblical and spiritual discussion will be going on. It will be a massive epic apocalyptic camp meeting of Biblical proportions, and a very noisy one at that. The prophet Micah said of regathered Jacob,

"They will make great noise by reason of the multitude of people". (Micah 2:12-13)

How long will this exile last? John the Revelator tells us precisely, to the very day. This time period for the exile is set for the final 3.5 years of this age. The Holy Spirit measures out this final 3.5 years of the age for us in very precise terms in seven different Bible verses.

The Bible refers to this final regathering of His covenant people using the word "Jacob". And so we know this includes the regathering of all 12 tribes of Greater 'Commonwealth of Israel' in their unrefined state. (See Eph.2:11-13) Our apostle Paul speaks of the Commonwealth, (or citizenship), of Israel as those who are called out of heathen gentile wickedness and come under the blood of Christ. Christians in the West are not told about this for fear of the secular princes of the West.

All of Jacob will be sequestered there at Bozrah. We must assume that this company of people includes multitudes of women and children. The body of the "Man-child" company will be born during this very same time period. The Great Tribulation period coincides with the travail of the woman and here at Bozrah we see her in her place of confinement. It is her birthing chamber even as the **body** of Man-Child company is about to be born at the First Resurrection. The sacred **Head** of the Man-child company was born 2,000 years earlier at the resurrection of Jesus Christ, on the morrow after the sabbath of Passover right on Resurrection Sunday on the Hebrew Feast of Firstfruits. Jesus our Messiah at His first coming was the Firstfruits from the dead even as the Head of the Man-Child was crowning and the birth began. The following Body of the Man-child company will be born as well. They are the key players on the stage of holy history during this climactic time. They will bring in the final 5th seal witness at the end of the age. They will finish the race on behalf of all of God's saints from both sides of Calvary.

It is true that many of the saints will die in the witness during those times. But they will be the ones given prominence in the Resurrection of the righteous dead which immediately precedes the Rapture at the end of the age. (See Revelation 20:4-6, and 1Thes. 4:15-17, and also 1Cor. 15:51-53) But the woman with the crown of 12 stars, though under great trial and travail, will be in confinement during this time before the Man-child is born at the Post-Tribulation Resurrection-Rapture. She will be taken off into exile at this "Bozrah" place during the entire period of regathering, refining, and restoration of Israel. The prophet Jeremiah said that this would be the time of "Jacob's Trouble". We know from cross referencing of Holy Scripture in the Olivet Discourse) that Jesus called this period of time following the abomination of desolation, the Great Tribulation'.

BIBLICAL TIME. 3.5 YEARS = 1260 DAYS THE TIME LOCK ON THE TRIBULATION PERIOD, AND A "ROSETTA STONE" FOR THE BIBLICAL YEAR.

The time period of this Bozrah exile, during which 'the woman' of Revelation 12 is nurtured is very precisely stated in Holy Scripture. (See **this video**.) To help ensure there is not any confusion about this, God has seen fit to state the time period for us twice in Revelation 12. In this same passage He gives us the time period for the flight and exile of His covenant people using **two different time units**. This is absolutely amazing! If our God, the Holy One of Israel took that extra effort to tell us **twice** what He intends to do at the end of the age then shouldn't we pay attention? God forbid that we continue to neglect this telling scripture and put a block on this very reassuring message of God's lovingkindness to His own during their latter day time of trial and tribulation. God is very definite about this. He says, **"I will gather ALL of you, Jacob"**.

Biblical Christians know that when the Seed of Abraham, (the indwelling Christ Himself), comes into their hearts and lives and takes up residence they become a "new creature". See 2Corinthians 5:17 and Galatians 6:15. We also know that our identity in Christ brings us into the 'Commonwealth of Israel'. (See Ephesians.2:11-13) So through the blood of Christ we become intimately identified with the Seed of Abraham.

So all that being understood, we as Christian believers should not try to pretend that this passage in Micah referring to "Jacob" is "just for the Jews", or "not for us", or "irrelevant to us as Christians in 'the Church' ".

These scriptures **are** for us!
And they **are** important!

THE FLIGHT OF THE WOMAN, (GOD'S COVENANT PEOPLE),
DURING THE TRIBULATION, THE FINAL 3.5 YEARS OF THIS
AGE, SEEN IN JOHN'S VISION OF REVELATION CHAPTER 12.

In Revelation 12:6 we are told that 'the woman' will be given "the wings of a great eagle" and that she will fly off to a place of safety where she can be nourished/fed for 1260 days. Eight verses late, in Revelation 12:14, we are given the very same information. The message is restated again. But this time it is given in terms of different time units. The time period for the exile of the woman is given in this verse as a "time, times, and half a time", or a period of **three and a half years**.

This is our "Rosetta stone" for prophetic time. It tells us in no uncertain terms what a 'year' means when the Ancient of Days dispenses His holy time to us in prophecies that come down to us from the courts of heaven. This is a clincher for Bible prophecy students as they co-relate the prophecies in Daniel and in the Book of Revelation. It "locks in" the time period of the latter half of the 70th Week of Daniel. The time period is given in two time units, those being days and biblical years. 1260 divided by 3.5 = 360. So the number of days in a biblical or prophetic year when a timed prophecy is issued from the courts of heaven is no longer in question. It is **360 days**.

God's covenant people in the end-time drama are showcased in scripture in several ways.
Jesus calls them 'the Elect' (singular) in the Olivet Discourse.
In Genesis and in Revelation 12 we also see them pictured as 'the woman'. They are also called the Commonwealth of Israel in Ephesians 2:11-13. They are called 'Jacob' in Micah 2:12-13. The prophet Micah states that they will be gathered in exile "as the sheep of Bozrah". (Mic. 12:12-13) Why is this flight to Bozrah necessary?

The Apostle John gives us the reason.
The 'woman'/Israel/the Church is being pursued by the

dragon.
She is given the wings of a great eagle.
And so she flees to pre-ordained a place of safety.
(Rev.12:6)

There at "her place" she will be protected and spiritually **nourished/fed**. (See Rev.12:6 & 12:14)
This exile lasts for a period of three and a half biblical years. (See Rev.12:14)
The time is also given as 1260 days. (See Rev.12:6)
This time of Jacob's Gathering we see in Micah 2:12-13 must surely be related to the great 666 rejection by God's covenant people which brings them into what the prophet Jeremiah called Jacob's trouble. This is also referenced in Holy Scripture as the time of the travail of the woman, again, another reference to God's covenant people from both houses of Israel. This epic period of time occurs during reign of the 666 Beast phase Antichrist when he is possessed by the Beast Demon of the Abyss and is revealed midway through the final seven years of this age as the Beast of 666. So this time of Great Tribulation occurs during the latter half of the 70th Week (or 70th seven), of Daniel 9:24-27. See **this chart of the future 70th Week of Daniel**. Jacob's gathering or the gathering of the remnant of Israel mentioned by the prophet Micah is the very same time period of 'Jacob's trouble'. And yes, the Church and Western Christendom are very much connected to Israel through the blood of Messiah. So contrary to what we have been told, Christian believers are in the loop. The blood of Christ brings them into the Commonwealth of Israel or the Citizenship of Israel.

Western Christians will be **heavily involved** in this epic latter day history. See **this short video**. Because while this epic exodus of God's 666 rejecting covenant people is taking place **some** group of saints at **some** time must eventually go up before the kings and rulers and bring in the 5th seal end-time witness. **Some** group of runners must finish the race on behalf of all the saints who have gone before them. If American and Western Christians are not prepared to consider this then they will have missed out on a great adventure and a divine romance in their God. And the God of Israel will raise up witnesses from another quarter. He will turn away from the contractor-grade carnal Christians of the West and rely on the higher grade blood covenant witness of faithful Chinese, Indonesian, Egyptian and a host of other Christian believers to do the job.

The end-time witness of the saints will not be a cakewalk.
The Valley of Decision will bring the days that try men's souls.
The prophet Jeremiah brings us both the somber news and the glorious news.
He tells us in one passage of Scripture.

Jeremiah 30
7. "Alas, for that day is great, so that none is like it.
And it is the time of **Jacob's Trouble,**
But he shall be saved out of it.

'Jacob's trouble' is the Great Tribulation period.
We could just as easily call it Jacob's Tribulation or the time of Jacob's Wrestling with God.

This period of time is abundantly documented in Holy Scripture.
(See Daniel 7:19-21 & 12:6-7.)

We see a 3.5 Biblical year, 42 Biblical month, 1260 day period.
It is the exact same time period of the trampling of Jerusalem, (See Rev.11:2).
It is the exact same time period ministry of the two witnesses, (See Rev. 11:3),
It is the exact same time period of the reign of the 666 Beast phase Antichrist. (See Daniel 12:6-7, Revelation 13:3-5.)

How did God's covenant people, the Jewish and Christian people get into this jam?
We know that the God of Israel is not capricious but righteous in all that He allows to happen.
Apparently 'the woman' before coming into her glory has been wanton, even as Gomer.
Moses gave a warning to God's people about this.
He told of the misbehavior of His people in the "latter days".
Moses prophesied that this waywardness in Jacob would come to some sort of a climactic head.
So did Jesus. (John 5:43)
God's covenant people have a humanistic inclination to take up with worldly lovers.

So here we see 'the woman', Israel, God's covenant people, in her final dalliance.
It will be her final and cataclysmic mistake.
She has made covenant with a false messiah.
She will give him her land and her sovereign power leaving herself with nothing.
In the manner of Esau she has sold her birthright for a mess of pottage.

Of course there are consequences to this.
She is now in a world of trouble.

But, all is not lost.
Something else of great wonder is happening.
And it is happening right inside the Tribulation period.
A great drama is unfolding during last half of the last seven years of this age.
The woman is in travail and in pain to be delivered.
She is also being threatened by the dragon empowering the 666 Antichrist.

Let us pause to take in the big picture here.
The **Head** of the Man-child has already been born.
He has already been resurrected to glory.
Jesus was the firstfruits from the dead. (1Cor. 15:20)
He rose from the dead and ascended to His Father nearly 2,000 years ago.
The **Body** of the Man-child is **next** to be born.
And all who are Christ's will be born into the glory as well. (1Cor. 15:23)
The Man-child is sacrificed in the drama of the 5th seal. (Rev.6:9-11)
Here the 'final witness' of the saints is brought before the courts of heaven.
John sees this great company gathering before the throne of God. (Rev. 12:5)
When it is complete God the Father will give the Word to wrap things up. (Rev. 16:1)

After the 5th seal and the 'final witness' of the saints comes the 6th seal. (Rev.6:12-13)
The heavens open and the sign of the Son of Man is seen in heaven. (Mat.24:30)

And the returning Messiah goes out to judge and to plead with the nations.
Then comes the final Day of Reckoning, the final 'Day of Atonement'. Immediately after the sun sets of that last day the Day of the Lord opens up and the great harvest of the end time is reaped. (Rev.14:14-20)

Meanwhile, the woman of Revelation 12 is in great travail. At the end of her confinement, (and the word "confinement" is a midwifery term"), she is being delivered of the Man-child. (Rev.12:1-2) She has been given the wings of a **great eagle**.

Remember, we have seen the covenant people of the God of Israel carried **"on eagles wings"** before. This was the poetic Biblical description of the exodus of Israel out of Egypt 3500 years ago. Now we hear the woman is given the wings of a **great eagle**. This mass airlift of people will be on a global operation carried out on a massive scale. It will be the most awesome stupendous airlift of people this world has ever seen.

Can we guess which nation or group of nations might be involved here?
Which nation or nations have the lion's share of the aircraft of the world?

The woman of Revelation 12, also referenced in Micah both as as regathered **"Jacob"** and **"the remnant of Israel"**, flees "into the wilderness" "away from the face of the dragon". (See Rev.12:6 and Rev. 12:14.) God, once again, is showing His great mercy in deliverance. And a certain country or group of countries is aiding the woman, the remnant of Israel, as she flies from the face of the Dragon. The flight of the woman has been fully provided for. She has been given the wings of a **great eagle**.

Of course others may have other ideas and another agenda. But the Holy Spirit through the Apostle John writes in the pages of Holy Scripture quite clearly that the woman is on her way to **"her place"**, a mystery place. And that place, wherever that geographical place turns out to be, is **"away from the face of the dragon"**. There, at **"her place"** the woman will be **"fed"** and **"nourished"**. For how long? Our Apostle Paul tells us **twice**. The exile of the woman will be for the last 3.5 years, (or 1260 days), of this age.

That final gathering place is identified in Micah 2:12-13 with the name 'Bozrah'.
Bozrah means 'sheepfold'. And this is our first major clue. God's covenant people will be regathered out of their worldwide dispersions and out of the Diaspora and penned up **together** in this mystery Bozrah place, the sheepfold of the Almighty.

Here is our next big clue.
In former times Bozrah was a pastoral city of Edom.
It belonged to the children of **Esau** .

THE PLACE OF THE EXILE IS GIVEN IN MICAH 2:12-13 AS BOZRAH.
IT IS NOT PETRA. PETRA WOULD NOT ACCOMMODATE MORE THAN 1,000 PEOPLE. FOR THOSE FLEEING JERUSALEM A REFUGE THERE WOULD BE A FATAL CHOICE.

WITH TODAY'S METHODS OF WARFARE PETRA WOULD BE A DEATH TRAP.

The name of the place of exile of then woman is given to us in scripture. It is **Bozrah**. And that is where the "Breaker" will come to deliver her at the end of the age. The place of refuge will not be Petra. There are **no** scripture passages that mention or allude to Petra. None!

So why the switch from Bozrah to Petra? Why hide the Bozrah scriptures with a troglodyte fable about Israel in the Tribulation finding shelter in Petra? Petra has never been able to accommodate more than 1,000 people. Clearly it is not big enough to shelter and supply food and other supplies for tens or hundreds of millions of people for three and a half years.

Petra is an unlikely, even impossible place, for an exile of the magnitude we see in Micah 2. Nor would it provide safe haven for the population of Judah and Jerusalem in the Armageddon scenario at the very end of the age. If we are considering a refuge for Israel in the Armageddon siege then we need to be brought up to date. Yes, in past times Petra was a retreat. The narrow passes into Petra were easily defended by men with bows and arrows and swords. But in these days of modern warfare the situation is far different. The modern government of Israel would never lead their people to Petra in Jordan for shelter. That deep gorge back in the days of the Edomite marauders was a good hide-out for a few hundred people. The deep and narrow entrance into the rock city was a good redoubt. But nowadays Petra would never qualify as a retreat. To put any population in there in these days of modern weapons would seal their doom. Petra would be a deathtrap.

And why? Because one big air burst fuel bomb down in that deep gorge would turn the whole canyon into an inferno. All the oxygen would be sucked out, just as we saw in the terrible firestorms of Hamburg and Dresden. The people in there would be incinerated or perish in their caves of suffocation. That would be the end of all the people in there. And with a chemical bomb the situation would be just as deadly. The gas would flow down the gorge and just sit there. a chemical gas attack in a gorge would kill the whole population. In the modern era of napalm and devilish chemical bombs a retreat to Petra would be absolutely suicidal. The gorge would soon become a fiery furnace and a valley of death. The supposed "refuge" would soon be a place of charred corpses. No one would survive.

So what is going on here with this "retreat to Petra" fable? Why do we continue to hear our Bibles teachers bring forth this improbable, even impossible, "Petra" story? And why has the much bigger Bozrah story we see in Micah 2:12-13 and Revelation 12:6 and 12:14 been hidden from the Church? Why have the Bozrah scriptures been "cloaked" by this unscriptural and fanciful "flight to Petra" story? Why did this Petra story get floated anyway? We keep hearing a lot about Petra whenever the Bozrah sheepfold issue is raised. But precious little in the way of a faithful plain reading exegesis of the Holy Scriptures as they pertain to this critically important prophecy of end-time Bozrah. Why the smokescreen? Why the misinformation? And why make up a Petra story when the word "Petra" is not even in the Bible? Just what is this little conflict in the information war all about? What is the agenda behind the disinformation here? That, dear saints, is what we shall be looking into as we proceed onwards in this article.

THE PLACE IS BOZRAH, NOT PETRA.
THE REAL STORY IS THE FLIGHT OF THE WOMAN, GOD'S ELECT, TO A PLACE OF EXILE AND NURTURING DURING THE TRIBULATION. THE BIBLE CALLS THIS PLACE BOZRAH AND IT IS PROBABLY A FARAWAY GEOGRAPHICAL LOCATION, OR A SET OF GEOGRAPHICAL LOCATIONS. BUT WHAT DO WE HEAR FROM OUR BIBLE TEACHERS? THE BOZRAH STORY IS BEING SWITCHED OUT. IT IS COVERED OVER BY A FALSE STORY ABOUT A SUPPOSED ESCAPE TO PETRA. THEY SAY THAT THE BOZRAH EXILE STORY IS REALLY A PETRA ESCAPE STORY AND THAT IT INVOLVES THE ESCAPE OF THE POPULATION OF JERUSALEM DURING THE EARTHQUAKE THAT SPLITS THE MOUNT OF OLIVES AT THE VERY END OF THE AGE. BUT THIS BELITTLES THE EPIC GRANDEUR OF THE BOZRAH EXILE AND THE BOZRAH DELIVERANCE.

The Bozrah story tells of a magnificent deliverance of God's people at the end of the age. It involves the exile in Bozrah of the covenant people of the God of Abraham, Isaac, and Jacob. And it refers to the return of Messiah at Bozrah as a Deliverer. The scriptures point to Bozrah as a place where the Elect are held during the time of "Jacob's trouble". They are held captive under the jurisdiction of the wild, untamed, and Godless children of Esau.

The Edomites are still with us today. An epic future time, the 70th Week of Daniel, will see them rise up just as Jacob prophesied. (Gen.27:39-40) They will be given dominion over God's covenant people. Micah sees the second coming of Messiah and the conclusion to the drama. He sees the Shepherd of Israel entering His sheepfold in the hours before dawn. Out there at Bozrah He becomes "the Breaker".

This wonderful Bozrah Deliverance prophecy is hidden. It is "cloaked" by the powers that be. A Bozrah deliverance presupposes a Bozrah exile. We are looking here at an incarceration of God's covenant people in the last 3.5 years of the age. This may be cross-referenced by John the Beloved as the flight of the woman of Revelation 12. This is very disturbing to some Christian believers. The rulers are well aware of past Church history. They probably fear that this information, (should it get out), may trigger societal disruptions by carnal Christians. And so at this point in time the entire Bozrah drama is under a religious smokescreen involving a so-called flight of latter day Judah in Israel to a supposed place of refuge in Petra. And so the real story of the Bozrah Exile is still an untold story.

Here below is the scripture in Micah that tells of the Bozrah exile and the Bozrah deliverance. This scripture is in the Old Testament. So its prophetic significance for the Church in the end time drama is missed. For reasons of political correctness this passage in Micah 2:12-13 is not addressed by today's teachers of Bible prophecy. Nor do they receive all the promises of lost Israel's restoration in the latter days as prophecy that might affect **them** as well as the regathering and restoration of the Jewish House of Judah. When YHVH-God says "I will regather and assemble **All of You**" He means just that!

He means that He will gather and restore **all 12 tribes of Israel!**

Micah 2
Hebrew Names Version of World English Bible

12. I will surely assemble, Ya`akov, all of you;
I will surely gather the remnant of Yisra'el;
I will put them together as the sheep of Botzrah,
As a flock in the midst of their pasture;
They will throng with people.

13. He who breaks open the way goes up before them.
They break through the gate, and go out.
And their king passes on before them,
With the LORD at their head."

Micah 2
King James Version

12. I will surely assemble, O Jacob, all of thee;
I will surely gather the remnant of Israel;
I will put them together as the sheep of Bozrah,
As the flock in the midst of their fold:

they shall make great noise
by reason of the multitude of men.

13. The breaker is come up before them:
they have broken up,
and have passed through the gate,
and are gone out by it:
and their king shall pass before them,
and the LORD on the head of them.
-Mic. 2:12-13 KJV

The image above shows a stone sheepfold of the type seen in biblical times. Here the sheep would be confined by their shepherd during the hours of darkness in a place of protection. As the dawn approached the shepherd would come into the sheepfold among His sheep. They would gather around the shepherd as he prepared to open a way for them to be delivered from the stone enclosure. As he opened a way out for them they would crowd up alongside him pushing against the gateway with a lot of force.

When the breakthrough came the whole flock would pour out of the sheepfold through the breach together with the Messiah as "the Breaker" going before them. They would follow on the heels of the Shepherd as he led them out to find pasture. This is the magnificent pastoral picture of the "man-child company" breaking forth into holy history at the end of the age. This will change the destiny of heaven and earth. The stars and angelic rulerships fall. And here on earth Messiah brings in His Millennial Kingdom. He will minister and rule for a thousand years.

This detailed picture of the deliverance of the elect **by Messiah** (and not the church) at the Second Advent is given to us in Micah chapter 2. This drama of the Bozrah Exile and Bozrah deliverance is laid out for us quite clearly and in detail.

The Bozrah deliverance is a thrilling element of the Second Coming of Christ. He is the Anointed One and our coming Messiah. The Micah 2 scripture shows the connection of the Second Coming of Christ to Bozrah, (an Edomite domain), very well. We also see The Bozrah deliverance laid out for us in spectacular fashion in **Isaiah 63.** This is the judgment side to the Second Coming of Christ. God is obviously telling us something here in these Bozrah scriptures. Each of them clearly relate to the return of Messiah.

BOZRAH, NOT PETRA.
THE "FLIGHT TO PETRA" IS BASED ON HUMAN SPECULATION.
THERE ARE NO REFERENCES TO PETRA IN THE BIBLE.
BUT THERE ARE MANY BOZRAH SCRIPTURES.

Unfortunately we do not get this story of the Bozrah Exile. Instead we get a "cover story" involving a supposed 'flight to Petra'. If evangelicals are going to present a story of a flight to Petra in the time of the Great Tribulation then where are the scriptures to support such a notion?

The short answer is this.
There are none!

THE SPLITTING OF THE MOUNT OF OLIVES AT THE SECOND COMING,
AND THE FLIGHT OF THE INHABITANTS OF JERUSALEM TO AZAL

Evangelical teachers who want to put a news blackout on this wonderful story of the Bozrah Exile and the eventual Bozrah deliverance do a bait and switch. They obfuscate and "cloak" the Bozrah prophecy. They throw in a substitute story about a supposed flight to Petra in the time of Armageddon and the second coming. They present the idea that Petra, an ancient city in Jordan would be a nice place of refuge for refugees coming out of Jerusalem during the big earthquake. This is the one that splits the Mount of Olives at the very end of this age. But it doesn't fit. There is no time for a prolonged exile here.

Well there will certainly be an epic earthquake that splits the Mount of Olives. And the inhabitants of Jerusalem will flee. But where will they flee to?
Are they really going to be Petra?

This "flight to Petra" notion is embedded in the evangelical family. Books have been written on it. And Biblical Christians bring it up quite often. It is brought up in relation to the trials of the Jewish people in Jerusalem at the end of the age and their flight out of the city of Jerusalem. But where did this idea of a "flight to Petra" in Jordan come from?

The scripture passage they present to support this is in Zechariah 14.

ZECHARIAH 14
1 Behold, the day of the Lord is coming,
And your spoil will be divided in your midst.
2 For I will gather all the nations to battle against Jerusalem;
The city shall be taken,
The houses rifled,
And the women ravished.
Half of the city shall go into captivity,
But the remnant of the people shall not be cut off from the city.
3 Then the Lord will go forth and fight against those nations,
As He fights in the day of battle.
4 And in that day His feet will stand on the Mount of Olives,

Which faces Jerusalem on the east.
And the Mount of Olives shall be split in two,
From east to west,
Making a very large valley;
Half of the mountain shall move toward the north
And half of it toward the south.

5 **Then you shall flee through My mountain valley,**
For the mountain valley shall reach to Azal.
Yes, you shall flee as you fled from the earthquake
In the days of Uzziah king of Judah.

Thus the Lord my God will come,
And all the saints with You.*

THE ESCAPE FROM THE EARTHQUAKE BY THE INHABITANTS OF JERUSALEM.

WHEN THE MOUNT OF OLIVES IS SPLIT THEY EVACUATE TO NEARBY AZAL

As we can see, there is no mention of Bozrah or Petra at all in this passage.
This is a flight of the inhabitants of Jerusalem out of the city during an earthquake.
That earthquake is the "big one" and it splits the Mount of Olives.
One element of the Second Coming is Jesus' return at the Mount of Olives.
He is the One who at His Second Coming causes the earthquake!

In this prophecy all the prophecies involving Edom there is no mention at all of the city of Petra.
And there is no mention of Petra in any other part of the Bible for that matter.
But here **is** a clear message of a flight out of Jerusalem that will end up in a nearby city.
That city is not way down in Jordan. It is in fact quite close to Jerusalem.
It is the **city of Azal**.

This "flight to Azal" happens at the very end of the age at the second coming of Christ.
The "flight to Azal" we see in the passage above is a short distance evacuation of Jerusalem.
The "flight to Azal" involves flight from an earthquake.
It occurs over a matter of hours and days.
It is not a prolonged exile over a period of years.
The passage gives no mention of a prolonged Tribulation refuge way down in Petra in Jordan.
This "flight to Azal" will not satisfy the prophecy of the

'flight of the woman' in Rev. 12:6 & 12:14.
Nor will not satisfy the scripture of the Bozrah exile and the Bozrah deliverance we see in Micah 2:12-13.

The so called "flight to Petra" is a hoax. It is a doctrine without any scriptural foundation whatsoever.
The 'Azal evacuation' scripture in Zechariah has been used to build up this Petra fable.
Then this "flight to Petra" and "refuge in Petra" fantasy is used in a "cover up".
The Petra refuge fable becomes a "cover story" for the real and solid prophecy of the Bozrah Exile.
Because we know that God will be gathering **all.** And we know that Messiah will be paying a visit to Bozrah at His Second Coming. (Isa. 63)

A RELIGIOUS SMOKESCREEN OVER THE BOZRAH EXILE.
AND A "CLOAKING" OF THE BOZRAH DELIVERANCE

Now we come to the next question. Why has this crucial information regarding the Bozrah exile and subsequent deliverance of God's elect from Edomite incarceration at Bozrah at the end of the age been "cloaked"? Why are we getting this Petra disinformation? What are the powers trying to do here? Just what is their agenda? Why have the Bozrah scriptures and the Revelation 12 scripture been omitted from teachings on end-time themes?

The Bozrah exile is a story of a rescue to a place of sanctuary during the great Tribulation is it not? The Bozrah deliverance one of the most exciting and inspiring

passages in the Bible. The Bozrah drama has obviously been put under a religious smokescreen by the religious powers. Why? Isn't the Bozrah story some exceedingly good and encouraging news?
So why haven't we heard this before?

Well it seems that when it comes to the question of the Great Tribulation Christian Bible teachers do not want to have to tell the Church they might be involved in any sort of exile. Even if it is outlined in the Bible in Micah 2:12-13 and in Revelation 12:6 and 12:14 they will studiously omit any reference to it as an end time scripture involving the Church. These dramas of the end-time, according to them, are not for the Church. They are "for the Jews". They tell us that this Great Tribulation, is the time of "Jacob's trouble". Therefore, according to them, the Great Tribulation will be a time of trial and tribulation for the Jews and the Jews only.

But is this true?
Is there any scriptural proof that the Church will not be here during the 70th Week?

Bible teachers know that the returning Messiah will deliver the inhabitants of Jerusalem when He comes back and His feet touch the Mount of Olives. When Jesus returns The Jewish nation and Jerusalem will be delivered from the end-time siege by the surrounding nations at Armageddon. - Zech.12:7-13:1 Christians know all about the deliverance of Israel at the Battle of Armageddon. But is this all there is to the Second Coming of Christ? Just what will the returning Christ be doing when He comes to Bozrah?

What Christians do **not** know is that at His Second Coming Christ will come in vengeance bringing wrath upon His enemies at Bozrah. (Isa.63) He will also deliver His saints at the same place, (or places), named in scripture as **Bozrah**. This is the awesome and magnificent Bozrah Deliverance.

Bozrah means "sheepfold". And it is a place under the end time sovereignty of Edom. These are two very valuable clues to the Bozrah story as it relates to the climax of this age. **Bozrah** is part and parcel of the end time drama. The exile to sanctuary in Bozrah and these deliverance actions by Messiah at Bozrah have not been taught by Bible prophecy teachers. But they are all part of the mosaic of this magnificent return of Messiah. Because He is coming back! And He will deliver and then glorify all His covenant people both in Israel and out in the nations. All this drama and adventure will be capped off at the **Resurrection-Rapture** at the end of the age.

The "cloaking" of this information about the Bozrah Exile is probably done with good intentions. It has been hidden from the Church at large. And it has been kept from them for their own good. The western Church is still immature. Even we as evangelicals are still a carnal, manipulative, and potentially violent people. So we probably did not deserve to know this Bozrah story.

But with this prophecy we are given hope. We don't need to be angry and violent. God has everything under control, even in the midst of Great Tribulation. According to Micah and the Apostle John our God will be merciful. He will nurture and feed His people **during** the Great Tribulation. He will take them a place of exile named Bozrah.

Bozrah has some connection to the Edomites we know. And the children of brother Esau will be in control. But if God says that the woman of Revelation 12 will be **"nurtured"** then some positive things will be going on. The remnant of all of the 12 tribes of Israel will be there. Micah says that all of Jacob will be gathered. (Micah 2:12-13). This will have to include the remnant of the lost 10 tribes.

And here is some more encouraging news. Just as in that former seven year famine back in Egypt, there will be "a famine of the hearing of the Word of God". (Amos 8:11) God's people will be hungry for spiritual truth. And the house of Joseph will be feeding them just as our patriarch Joseph did in the former time. The House of Joseph will be there. And once again Joseph will be laying out a table for his brethren. And he will be revealing some mysteries, even in the midst of tears. All this will happen in the Bozrah Exile.

So is this Bozrah prophecy all bad? Just what will be happening during the Tribulation period out at the sheepfolds of Bozrah?

Quite clearly the Bozrah exile will not just be an incarceration story. Apparently the Bozrah enclosure also provide some degree of **shelter** and even **nurturing or spiritual nourishment** for the children of Abraham, Isaac, and Jacob in the end-time. Bozrah is in fact a place of relative safety.

THE FLIGHT TO BOZRAH AND THE GATHERING OF ALL OF JACOB IN MICAH 2:12-13.
AND THE FLIGHT OF THE WOMAN OF

REVELATION 12:8 & 12:14.
THEY ARE ONE AND THE SAME

To pick up the rest of the story we shall now go to the apocalypse of John. In the saga of 'the woman of Revelation 12' we see the story of the flight of the woman, (a picture of God's covenant people), "away from the face of the dragon". She is obviously taken off to a place of exile. And the **time** of this exile corresponds to the time of the latter half of the 70th Week of Daniel, the final 3.5 years of this age. This is the time of the Great Tribulation and the trampling of Jerusalem.

Why is the woman in exile for three and a half years?
As we study the scripture passage in Revelation 12 we see that she is there for two purposes.

1. She is there to be protected. And
2. She is there to be nurtured.

This must mean a spiritual nurturing or nourishment. She will be physically cared for too it seems. This prophecy of the woman who takes flight on the wings of an eagle to a place of nurturing for the exact time period of the Great Tribulation is clearly telling us a very important part of the story of the end-time. It parallels the story of the exile of the children of Abraham, Isaac, and Jacob in the end-time at Bozrah. Bozrah is the place, (or places), where Jacob can be nurtured in the things of God. This will be happening during the last half of the 70th week, and during the time of the Great Tribulation.

The Bozrah story cannot be hidden forever. It will be told eventually. Bozrah is an important spiritual place in which God will protect, preserve, refine, and nurture His people in the end-time drama.

Where will end-time Bozrah be located? Right now we do not know where Bozrah might be geographically. It may be many places. Or it may be one place. It may be one central dumping ground for Judeo-Christian troublemakers in the latter days.

Oh yes, the Bozrah scriptures do not just refer to "past history". Nor is Bozrah just an archeological dig on a ruin of an ancient pastoral city of Esau southeast of the Dead Sea. For those who are there at this appointed place in the latter days this will be the place the prophets Isiah and Micah spoke about. Bozrah will be a very real place under the control of modern day Edomites. It may well turn out to be a geo-political area far from the Promised Land. It may be a modern geo-political area out at the ends of the earth. The covenant people of God may look up in those days to find themselves in the place the Old Testament prophets spoke of over 2700 years ago.

And there, in that place they will find their God. They will find Him

"...as rivers of water in a dry place,
as the shadow of a great Rock in a weary land." (Isa.32:2)

-o-o-o-o-o-o-o-o-o-o-o-o-o-o-o-o-o-o-o-o-o-o-o-o-o-o-o-o-o-o-o-o-o-

And that is where Messiah,
Will find them at the end.

A day of wrath, deliverance;
"The Breaker" comes to rend,

He comes to make the breakthrough,
His sheep are pressing in;
He leads them out, they follow Him,
And on 'that Day' they win!

All of this will happen;
At the sheepfolds of Bozrah. -Mic.2:12-13

THE BOZRAH DELIVERANCE.

MICAH 2:12-13

The End-Time **Flight to Bozrah** during the final 3.5 years of this age and the ensuing **Bozrah Exile** during the Great Tribulation, is a subject that is almost never spoken about by Bible teachers. But this is laid out in the Holy Scriptures quite clearly in Micah 2:12-13 and Revelation 12. And now the subject of the magnificent **Bozrah Deliverance** by our returning Messiah is no longer cloaked and under wraps. It is in fact going viral as we see in this video below. There will be a great parting of the ways and an epic division of people during the 666 economic system of the Antichrist. Those who reject the 666 system of marking will be on the outer.
What about the women and the children? Is all lost? No. Apparently not.

Micah 2
King James Version

The Exile
12. I will surely assemble, O Jacob, all of thee;

I will surely gather the remnant of Israel;
I will put them together as the sheep of Bozrah,
As the flock in the midst of their fold:
they shall make great noise
by reason of the multitude of men.

The Deliverance
13. The Breaker is come up before them:
they have broken up,
and have passed through the gate,
and are gone out by it:
and their king shall pass before them,
and the LORD on the head of them.
-Mic. 2:12-13 KJV
(The word 'Breaker' is capitalized by GWF
since there are no capitals in the original Hebrew
and we are surely looking here at the coming Messiah.)

SUMMARY:

The Bible paints a picture of a magnificent deliverance at the end of the age. It involves the returning Messiah and the covenant people of the God of Abraham, Isaac, and Jacob. The scriptures point to Bozrah as a place where the Elect, God's covenant people, are in exile. It is the time of "Jacob's trouble". From the Bozrah connection to Edom it appears that they are held under the jurisdiction of the wild, untamed, and Godless children of Esau. The Edomites are still with us today. An epic future time, the 70th Week of Daniel, will see them rise up just as Jacob prophesied. (Gen.27:39-40) They will be given dominion over God's covenant people. Micah sees the second coming of Messiah and the conclusion to the drama. He sees the Shepherd of Israel entering His sheepfold in the hours before dawn. Out there at Bozrah He becomes "the Breaker".

This wonderful prophecy of the Bozrah Deliverance is there in our Bibles. But it remains hidden. It is "cloaked" by the powers that be. The Bozrah deliverance would be quite problematical for the western church to address since it presupposes a preceding Bozrah exile. It also leaves us to wonder about an earlier 'flight to Bozrah' by God's covenant people in what must be a future exodus involving an epic airlift of hundreds of millions of people. This latter day mega-event would be a great and awesome migration of Biblical proportions.

John the Apostle tells us in Revelation 12 that this gathering or sheltering of God's covenant people is for their nurturing and their feeding. Surely a spiritual feeding is in view here as well as physical care and the sustaining of human life.. Micah in Micah 2:12-13 refers to the 'sheepfold of Bozrah". But only the KJV and Young's Literal Translation have allowed this information to pass through to us. Unfortunately this reference to the "Bozrah sheepfold" is not to be found in the modern translations. It seems to have been "lost in translation". Search the passages presented to us in the modern versions of the Bible and you will not find the word "Bozrah". Guardians of the religious status-quo in those translation committees apparently saw fit to leave it out. Why? We shall look into this matter further.

In Revelation 12:6 and 12:14 we see quite clearly that this end-time exile will be going on during the last 3.5 years or 1260 days of this age. So the Micah 2:12-13 passage concerning the gathering of Jacob, (God's covenant people before they are refined to become Israel, - Prince with God), cross references with John's account of the flight and exile of the woman in Revelation 12. John saw the woman in travail being delivered of the man-child. This is precisely what we would expect in the end-time drama. This is clearly an apocalyptic event since the 1260 day/3.5 year time period coincides exactly with the Great Tribulation. Jesus tells us that this Great Tribulation will come after the midweek abomination of desolation which is half way through the 70th Week of Daniel, the final seven years of this age.

So we have two perspectives on this magnificent story, one from the Old Testament and one from the New Testament. The dramas involving Bozrah in Micah 2:12-13 may be cross-referenced in the message John the Beloved brings to us in Revelation 12:13-17. Here in this passage we see the end-time flight of the woman.

The suggestion of an exile of Christian believers in the final seven years of this age would be very disturbing for most. And so the fact of the matter is that most Christians are being deliberately misinformed about these important matters. This information is being blocked or censored out. Christians know that some group of saints will finish the race at the end of the age. (Heb.12:1) But they are being told that these future saints will not and cannot be them. They are not being told the real story about the late Resurrection-Rapture. They are not being spiritually prepared by the church for the end-time witness of the saints.

This is understandable. These hidden pearls of Biblical truth should not be handed out to the profane religious crowds. Most Christians in the west are only nominal in their faith. And we, as evangelicals, are for the most part living on the carnal side of our nature right now. The Bozrah Deliverance is truly a magnificent future event. But such knowledge is too wonderful for us it seems. The thought of an exile cannot be received by most Christians today without them responding in fear and hiding. Many Biblical Christians will be offended by this call to witness and inclined to follow some pied piper espousing some sort of militant violent nationalism. Some may shake their fist at God, declare a "raw deal", throwing down their Bibles go off into apostasy. Many will rage off onto the low road of personal survivalism and down a pathway that leads to tragedy.

Here is the truth of the matter. Many Christians in America are armed. If their constitutional freedoms are threatened they become very fearful and may be inclined to act out politically and also perhaps in unpredictable ways. And so if the true and Biblically correct end-time truth was to be taught openly from the pulpits it could prove to be socially disruptive. Disgruntled unprepared uninformed Christians could become violent in their actions, particularly as the climax of the age drew near. So if this sensitive Biblical information must be kept under wraps right now perhaps it is for the best. The true saints like the noble Bereans in past times will not be dissuaded by disinformation. They will seek out and find the truth. When the trials come the wise will not be caught unawares. Nor will they be surprised like the wicked when that Day sneaks up on them like a thief in the night. They will search the scriptures for themselves. Those who are wise will know what they are called to do and do it. Then, under the power and the guidance of the Holy Spirit they will respond to these hard sayings honorably and faithfully. These are the committed saints, the sold-out ones. These people, Christian believers from all nations, are special. They do what they do out of love and devotion. They are in a blood covenant relationship as a Bride to her Bridegroom. They sign on the dotted line, right there on the same document with their Messiah. They are on the spiritual battlefield campaigning with the Word of God and intercession under the guidance of the Holy Spirit. They are out there in the field and their lives are on the line. So they **deserve** to be "in the know".

The secular and ecclesiastical rulers are well aware of the dangers of Bible Prophecy. Messages on the Second Coming of Christ are strictly banned from the government regulated "Three Self" Church in China. There are not any Bible readings on the Second Coming of Christ in the liturgy of the Church of England. The Church in the west seems to have deliberately set out to either exclude or distort Bible Prophecy. Faithful Bible teachers have been pushed aside in favor of motivational speakers geared towards pleasing the "me-first" generation.

There are reasons for this, some good, and some bad. First of all soporific religion is what the crowds and deacon boards want. It is popular and revenue positive. The powers are also committed to maintaining peace and order. So they think that this is best achieved by downplaying any new Christian movements and upholding the status quo. The second reason is Church leaders do not like change. They remember the stormy periods of past Church history. The bloody mayhem in central Europe during the Reformation was a sad chapter in our past. The Amish and Mennonites remember it as well. If you ask them about what happened back then to the Anabaptists they will tell you. The rulers are concerned that end-time truth, including this Bozrah Deliverance story, (should it get out), may trigger a repeat of the awful civil and societal disruptions seen in times past.

Their fears are probably well founded. Carnal Christians have caused considerable trouble, even bloody mayhem, in days gone by. And firebrand Christians could certainly rise up again in the turbulent times of trial that lie up ahead. And so at this point in time the entire Bozrah drama, wonderful and inspiring as it is, remains an untold story. It is "cloaked" and under a religious smokescreen.

It is easy to see how this state of affairs goes on. The sheep of God's pasture are being fleeced but all too often are not being fed. Most Christians have no idea that they are a part of **'the woman'** we see showcased in Holy Scripture from Genesis to Revelation. Nor do born again Christians realize that they are no longer heathen gentiles. As "new creatures" they have a "new citizenship" and through the blood of Christ they have entered into the Commonwealth of Israel. See this passage in Ephesians 2:11-13. The Seed of Abraham, the indwelling Christ, has come inside "born again" Christians to make them new creatures. Our Apostle Paul has also spoken on this matter of the Seed of Abraham in Galatians 3:29. And in Romans 11 we see the final salvation and regathering of the whole family of Greater Israel. As Paul says, "And so **All Israel** shall be saved".

This is a magnificent element to the story of the end-time restoration of Israel. But the flight of 'the woman' to a place of refuge in Bozrah is virtually unknown in

Christendom. It has been hidden. The true and genuine 'flight to Bozrah' story has been crafted, re-engineered, and downsized into a much lesser story. In the place of Bozrah we have have been given a cover story. It involves to rock city of Petra in Jordan. We hear a story of a supposed 'flight of the Jews in Jerusalem to Petra' at the end of the age. But this is just a religious fable and it is "small potatoes" compared to the massive Bozrah prophecy we see in Micah 2.

The prophet Micah speaks about this huge end time gathering and exile of the saints at Bozrah.
The prophecy is laid out for us here in Micah 2:12-13.

But unfortunately this Bible passage is ignored by our Bible prophecy teachers. They do not dare touch it because of the hope and encouragement it gives for Christians who are just now beginning to understand their vital blood covenant role of witness in the 70th Week of Daniel.

And so this splendid salvation and deliverance story remains unknown. The prophet Isaiah also spoke about Bozrah in Apocalyptic tones and language. He spoke about the return of Messiah in wrath on His enemies and in deliverance of His saints.

And where will this epic deliverance take place?
At Bozrah. (See Isaiah 63).
But to this day it remains an untold story.

THE SHEEPFOLD OF BOZRAH,
THE IMPLIED EXILE OF THE WOMAN OF ISRAEL

AT BOZRAH.
AND THE END TIME DELIVERANCE OF THE ELECT

The Bozrah deliverance is a story of great wonder. And yet it has not been spoken about. Christian Bible teachers are not expounding on this good news of the end time. And we are not hearing about it from the pulpit or Christian television.

The Bozrah deliverance is truly extraordinary. It is the climax of a series of events that some Christian and Messianic Bible students believe will occur at the end of this age. Bozrah is the scene of a spectacular break-out. The deliverance of God's single undivided Elect is performed by none other than our own Messiah.

This is amazing. How will this deliverance happen? Let us back up and take in the earlier events that led up to this. At the end of the age God's covenant people are off in some place of exile or incarceration. This epic 'break out' at Bozrah is cross referenced in Isaiah 62. So the climax of the Bozrah story is prophesied to occur at Christ's second coming. See Micah 2:12-13 and Isaiah 63 Day of the Lord will open up and the heavens will be unrolled as a scroll. This epic day of wrath and deliverance follows immediately after the final wrap-up Day of Reckoning or Day of Atonement which is the seventh of the Seven Feasts of Israel.

After the judgment of the wicked and the deliverance of the Elect Messiah will judge the nations at the Sheep-Goat Judgment. (Mat.25) Then He will establish up His Millennial Kingdom. So as we can see, the details of these Apocalyptic events at Bozrah can be pieced together from key passages in the Old Testament prophecies of Isaiah 63, Micah 2:12-13, as well as the prophecy of the flight of the woman, God's covenant people, in Revelation chapter 12.

To understand the Bozrah deliverance some background information from the Bible is necessary. An understanding of the meaning of the word 'Bozrah' and its implications is absolutely crucial here. 'Bozrah' means 'sheepfold'. Bozrah was a pastoral city of Edom east of the Dead Sea. But there is more. The Edomite sovereignty over the city of Bozrah is an exceedingly important issue here as well. Because from what we see in the **prophecy of Isaac over Esau** the children of Esau, the godless Edomites, are prominent players in the end time drama. This is another vital truth about the end-time that virtually no-one, not even in evangelical circles, is speaking about.

And so here is a main lesson to be understood. The name and character of Bozrah belongs to Edom, the children of godless Esau. And that is how it will be in the end time drama. Bozrah is apparently a place geographically far removed from the Middle East and the international action we see there when the Dragon sends his armies west towards Jerusalem. We know for a certainty that Bozrah will be far "away from the face of the dragon". So Mystery Bozrah will probably be a place, (or places), out at the ends of the earth.

The Edomite name and character of Bozrah in the latter days is critical information. This cannot be over-emphasized. Esau was the wild hunting hustling brother of the nurturing family man, the patriarch Jacob. Jacob's concern was always for the tents of his fathers and a nurturing of the flocks. Even if Jacob was somewhat of a "heel" and a grasper and a trickster his heart was for the family of the promise. The other brother, Esau was untamed and ungodly. He was a hunter and a hustler, a "take you down" sort of a guy. The Bozrah deliverance completes the story of these two wrestling brothers. The Bozrah Deliverance brings it all right through to its epic climax in the Apocalypse.

JACOB AND ESAU HAVE WRESTLED WITH EACH OTHER FROM THE BEGINNING.
THE STRUGGLE COMES TO ITS EPIC CONCLUSION AT THE END OF THE AGE.

Here is some background information on Jacob and Esau. These two sons of Isaac were twins. They began wrestling with each other when they were still within their mother Rebekah's womb. When she inquired of God as to the cause of this awful wrestling within her she was told that the twins within her womb would become two nations.

Jacob and Esau have been wrestling with each other for approximately 4,000 years. Apparently this wrestling will come to an epic climax at some point in holy history. And here in the Bozrah story we find out when and where this will all come down. The wrestling will end with the return of Messiah ... at Bozrah.

Jacob and Esau grew up together, sons of Isaac and Rebekah. The two were quite different in character. Jacob was a nurturing, person, a man of the flocks. There was a dark side to his early character development. This is embodied in the name, 'Jacob', which means 'heel grasper', 'trickster', or 'supplanter'. Nevertheless Jacob's place was as a caregiver, shepherd, and husbandman. And there at home with family at the homestead he immersed himself in the faith of his fathers. Eventually, after going through many trials his pilgrimage will take him to a threshold and through a strait gate. As the patriarchal and prophetic story unfolds Jacob does indeed undergo a character change. And so he gets an appropriate name change. After the death of Rachel and the birth of his last son Benjamin, which means "son of my right hand" Jacob becomes Israel, which means "prince with God".

Esau was quite different. He was a hunter and a wild man. He was a free-ranging spirit of the open field, open minded, open to anything and everything. Esau had little time for the narrow way, the life at home and for the God of his fathers Abraham and Isaac. Esau was a rover. He eventually took a foreign Canaanite wife and worshiped foreign gods bringing his parents and his family much grief.

Jacob began his heel grasping ways by stealing Esau's birthright. He also deceived his father. He tricked his brother Esau out of the blessing that was due him as the firstborn. When Esau realized the full implication of what had happened he went to his father weeping. Esau asked if there was any blessing left over for him.

Well there was. And this is the big story that has been all but forgotten by Bible teachers today. Isaac gave his eldest son Esau a leftover blessing. Yes, Esau would become restless and break loose of the bonds of civility and law and order to be given dominion over Jacob in the latter days. This **must** be a reference to the Bozrah exile in the latter days.

Jacob's blessing over Esau has **huge** implications for the Judeo-Christian peoples as they come into the arena of the end-time drama. Let us look at the details here. Isaac pronounced a prophecy over his eldest son. He said that Esau would eventually become restless. Eventually the time would come when Esau's children would rise up against the peaceful rule of the nurturing children of Jacob. Esau would break the yoke from around his neck and cast loose all civilized constraints. Jacob's yoke (of peaceful submission) would be broken from off his neck.

Dear saints, this is an extremely significant prophecy. God is telling us what will happen in the latter days. As we look all around us in our society and in the popular culture today we realize that this is already starting to happen. There is a wild and angry culture of godlessness abroad. Just step into the bookstore or video store and look at the images and titles. This culture of godlessness is now expanding and beginning to gain the upper hand. Is this resurgent fleshly nature the spirit of Esau at work? Isn't this declension of godliness and civility something we are seeing on a major scale now as we approach the end of this age?

The resurgence of the Edomites in the end-time is an untold story. We should not be surprised or unduly alarmed about all this. It provides some explanation for the present day moral meltdown in the west. It also provides the background information for the Bozrah exile and the Bozrah deliverance. God said that Esau would rise up. And so we must face up to it. Here is the scripture passage showing us Isaac's blessing over his eldest son Esau.

GENESIS 27
39 Then Isaac his father answered and said to him:
"Behold, your dwelling shall be of the fatness of the earth,
And of the dew of heaven from above.
40 By your sword you shall live,
And you shall serve your brother;
And it shall come to pass, **when you become restless, That you shall break his yoke from your neck.**"
-Gen.27:39-40

The implication of this prophecy is that Esau will be greatly blessed in riches and blessings. But that eventually he will run wild. The wild and brutish sons of Esau, the Edomites, have not disappeared into history. They must still be here with us and alongside us if God is going to deal with them decisively at Bozrah. The children of Esau will emerge into history in a big way. So much so that Messiah has to come to a place the Bible calls Bozrah and deal with the Edomites decisively as history comes to its climax. This was clearly prophesied by the prophet Isaiah in that awesome passage of scripture, Isaiah 63.

The Edomites were always an untamed, predatory, and godless race of people. The prophecy in Esau's blessing suggests that the children of Esau will erupt into history. They will break free of constraint as this age comes to its tumultuous and climactic conclusion. King David also alluded to this casting loose of the bonds of submission to God's righteous law. He tells us about it in the song he wrote in Psalm 2. The prophet Daniel, in Daniel 11:41 confirms this as well. He indicates that Edom, the children of Esau, will become restless and run wild. They will even escape the control of the coming Antichrist.

THE END-TIME DRAMA, AND THE RETURN OF MESSIAH AS
"THE BREAKER" COMING IN WRATH AND DELIVERANCE, AT BOZRAH.

One important aspect of the Second Coming of Christ is the arrival of Messiah at a place identified in the Old Testament as Bozrah. This is a place in the sphere of Edom, the children of Esau. The name Bozrah means "sheepfold" and this along with its Edomite connection provides the reason for the return of Messiah to Bozrah. Messiah is coming in wrath on His enemies and deliverance of His Elect people. Bible students are beginning to discuss the implications of this Bible prophecy. Isaiah and Micah both prophesy that the coming Messiah is coming to judge the wicked and deliver His covenant people at a place or places identified prophetically as Bozrah.

The prophet Isaiah in Isaiah 63 shows the returning Messiah in graphic prophetic poetry. He is trampling His enemies on the Day of Judgment. The place of this divine wrath is out at Bozrah which was the pastoral territory of Esau's sheepfolds. Apparently a protectorate of Edom known as Bozrah will be a place of God's visitation for judgment of the wicked and deliverance of the Elect at the end of the age. The returning Messiah will punish the wicked there. It will be similar to the sort of divine Messianic judgment Zechariah has prophesied will be carried out against the armies of the nations threatening Jerusalem from the Valley of Armageddon.

But the Bozrah scriptures tell more than just a story of divine wrath on God's enemies. Out at Bozrah there will also be a dramatic prison breakout. The returning Messiah will deliver His covenant people from incarceration by Esau. Apparently they will be penned up at a place or places identified prophetically as Bozrah. The prophet in Micah 2:12-13 identifies the coming Messiah as "the Breaker". This means that the returning Messiah will be breaking something. What might that be?

We are not left to guess here. The pastoral scene is well known. When Messiah returns He acts in mercy and deliverance. The Shepherd of Israel breaks His people out.

Breaks His people out?
Breaks them out from what?

The answer is quite clear.
Our returning Messiah breaks them out of Esau's sheepfold.

Bozrah is apparently a place of exile. Bible students are not constrained to believe that Bozrah at the end of days has to necessarily be located in the same geographical area of the ruins of ancient city of Bozrah southeast of the Dead Sea. From the apocalyptic nature of the Bozrah passages in Isaiah 63 and Micah 2 it seems clear that the place will appear on some map in the latter days. But just where is a subject for speculation. The Bozrah Isaiah and Micah saw will certainly be controlled by the Edomites of the latter day. The same wild hustling children of Esau will be on the scene. They will be giving the children of Abraham, Isaac and Jacob grief and correction just as they did in former times.

Isaiah sees the returning Messiah dealing with His enemies. He will crush them in a military sort of way just as described in Isaiah 63. The prophet Micah picks up the dramatic rescue element to the Bozrah story. He shows Messiah in His deliverance role. He has allowed His remnant covenant people to be penned up in Esau's sheepfold. He has done this for their protection and their nurturing. (See the article on 'The Woman and the Dragon of Revelation 12.

Messiah is no absentee God. Here at the end of the age we see Him returning to those of His people who are in exile under Edomite dominion out at Bozrah.

The pastoral imagery here is striking to those who know shepherding. The dawn of a new day is approaching. The returning Christ/Messiah enters the sheepfold as "the Breaker". His sheep are pressing in all around Him. He then makes His way to the wall of the sheepfold and breaks open a Way or a gate. For a short moment the Messiah as the Breaker is the Door of the sheepfold. He breaks His people out of Esau's enclosure in the same manner as a shepherd opens a doorway in a stone sheepfold at dawn. The shepherd then leads his sheep out to pastures and into a new day. These are the pastoral elements to the story of the magnificent Bozrah deliverance. The picture is very clear in the Hebrew poetry. It is a glorious yet untold element of the Second Coming of Christ. Because Messiah, when He returns, will be coming to His sheepfold as **'The Breaker'**.

Here below is the scripture. This scripture is in the Old Testament. So its prophetic significance is missed. It is rarely, if ever, mentioned by today's teachers of Bible prophecy.

Micah 2
Hebrew Names Version of World English Bible

12. I will surely assemble, Ya`akov, all of you;
I will surely gather the remnant of Yisra'el;
I will put them together as the sheep of Botzrah,
As a flock in the midst of their pasture;
They will throng with people.

13. He who breaks open the way goes up before them.
They break through the gate, and go out.
And their king passes on before them,
With the LORD at their head."

Micah 2
King James Version

12. I will surely assemble, O Jacob, all of thee;
I will surely gather the remnant of Israel;
I will put them together as the sheep of Bozrah,
As the flock in the midst of their fold:
they shall make great noise
by reason of the multitude of men.

13. The breaker is come up before them:
they have broken up,

*and have passed through the gate,
and are gone out by it:
and their king shall pass before them,
and the LORD on the head of them.*
-Mic. 2:12-13 KJV

The image above shows a stone sheepfold of the type seen in biblical times. Here the sheep would be confined by their shepherd during the hours of darkness in a place of protection. As the dawn approached the shepherd would come into the sheepfold among His sheep. They would gather around the shepherd as he prepared to open a way for them to be delivered from the stone enclosure. As he opened a way out for them they would crowd up alongside him pushing against the gateway with a lot of force. This is the same picture spoken of by Matthew in that difficult and problematic verse in Matthew 11:12.

"The Kingdom of God suffers (allows) violence
and the violent (are pressing in to) take it by force."
(Mat.11:12)

When the breakthrough came the whole flock would pour out of the sheepfold through the breach together with the Messiah as "the Breaker" going before them. They would follow on the heels of the Shepherd as he led them out to find pasture. This is the magnificent pastoral picture of the "man child company" breaking forth into holy history at the end of the age. This will change the destiny of heaven and earth. The stars and angelic dominions will fall. And here on earth Messiah brings in His Millennial Kingdom. He will minister and rule for a literal one thousand years.

This detailed picture of the deliverance of the Elect **by Messiah** (and not by the Dominionist church) comes at the

Second Advent. This message of hope is given to us in Micah chapter 2. The drama begins with the gathering of Jacob, (which includes the both houses of Unrefined Israel). The true and genuine Church will eventually come to realize their identity in the Commonwealth of Israel. This gathering leads to the Bozrah exile and then culminates with the Bozrah deliverance. This sequence of events is laid out for us quite clearly and in detail in Micah 2:12-13.

Note well that the Second Coming of Christ is what brings the breakthrough here and not a Dominionist Church. Our Messiah is the Deliverer here. He and He alone is "the Breaker". No churchman will get Messiah's glory here even if he claims some super-anointed status in the charismatic "five-fold ministry" and pretends to be up to the task of bringing in the Kingdom Now. Neither today's "apostolic/prophetic", nor the Papal/Jesuit Catholic leaderships can fit the bill here. Nor can today's political Puritan leaders or political Ecumenical leaders bring in the final breakthrough. Such actions in the flesh lead only to the Ecclesiastic harlotry John saw in Revelation 17. No crusading religious champions can lay claim to this end time glory. Jesus Christ/Yeshua Hamashiach is our Savior and our Redeemer. He is also our future Deliverer. Man cannot do this. The scriptures declare unequivocally that there is one and only one intermediary between God and man, the man Christ Jesus.

1 TIMOTHY 2
5 "For there is one God, and one mediator between God and men,
the man Christ Jesus;
6 Who gave himself a ransom for all, ..."

He and He alone is **"the man"**. No one else is capable of filling His shoes.

The Bozrah deliverance is a thrilling element of the Second Coming of Christ. He is the Anointed One and our coming Messiah. The Micah 2 scripture shows the connection of the Second Coming of Christ to Bozrah, (an Edomite domain), very well. We also see The Bozrah deliverance laid out for us in spectacular fashion in **Isaiah 63.** This is the judgment side to the Second Coming of Christ. God is obviously telling us something here in these Bozrah scriptures. Each of them clearly relate to the return of Messiah.

Why has this crucial information regarding the deliverance of God's elect from Edomite incarceration at the end of the age been omitted from teachings on end-time themes? Is this not some exceedingly good and encouraging news? Why haven't we heard this before?

The Old Testament is absolutely full of inspiring millennial poetry. God's holy Word is in concert together bringing us different elements of the same message of the Second Coming of Christ. There will be a great turnaround at the end of the age. This is exceedingly good news. It is dramatic and inspiring beyond measure. Yet many Christians have not heard this before. Why might this be?

Well it seems that Christian leaders today prefer to keep the emphasis on "The Church". They are the "New Testament people". These dark dramas of the end-time are "for the Jews". This is "Jacob's trouble". It will be trouble for the Jews and the Jews only we have been told. But is this entirely true?

Here are the facts of Holy Scripture. God will surely deliver "all" of His hard pressed people from out of captivity at the end of this age. He will come in the clouds and this is well known by evangelicals today in the rapture context. They also know that He will also deliver our Jewish brethren when He comes at the Mount of Olives. When Jesus returns He will deliver the Jewish nation from the end-time siege by the surrounding nations at Jerusalem. - Zech.12:7-13:1 Christians know about Armageddon. Is this all there is to the Second Coming of Christ? Is there more?

What Christians do **not** know is that at His Second Coming Christ will also come in vengeance upon His enemies and He will deliver His saints at a place, (or places), known as **Bozrah. All** of this is part and parcel of the **Resurrection-Rapture** seen at the end of the age.

The glorious Millennium of Messiah will follow this end-time deliverance precisely as the scriptures have laid out for us.

1 "Even the wilderness will rejoice in those days.
The desert will blossom with flowers.
2 Yes, there will be an abundance of flowers and singing and joy!
The deserts will become as green as the mountains of Lebanon,
as lovely as Mount Carmel's pastures and the Plain of Sharon.
There the LORD will display his glory, the splendor of our God.
3 With this news, strengthen those who have tired hands, and encourage those who have weak knees.
4 Say to those who are afraid,

"**Be strong, and do not fear,
for your God is coming to destroy your enemies.
He is coming to save you.**" -Isa 35:1-4

At this point, here is the question we need to ask ourselves. Are the Edomites, those godless children of Esau still with us today? Were they scattered into the nations as the Jewish nation was in the Diaspora? And if they are going to coalesce and regroup into some sort of a power force in the rich nations of the earth and dominate the nurturing people of Jacob just what role are they going to play in the end time drama?

Here is what the scriptures are telling us. The Edomites, it seems, are still with us. They are all around us; fellow citizens in our nations. Indeed they are very prominent players at the end of the age. Even the Antichrist will not conquer them or rule over them during the regime of the 666 system. (Dan. 11:41) Apparently he will not even bother to mess with them during the **Great Tribulation**, those **final 3.5 years** of this age. He will allow them to do what Edomites do. Create chaos in society that calls for a crackdown, even martial law. **End-Time Esau will rise up in the end time and achieve mastery over his brother Jacob** just as Isaac prophesied. This is the hidden information and extremely important for us to know about and prepare our hearts for. But it is being kept from the saints.

The "cloaking" of this information about End-Time Bozrah is probably done with good intentions. It has been hidden from the Church at large and it has been kept from them for their own good. The western Church is still immature and shielded from Biblical truth. Christians in the West for the most part are still a carnal and potentially violent people. According to **Micah 2** God will allow this exile and incarceration of His covenant people to proceed. And in Revelation 12:6 and 12:14 we see that this will go on for the limited time of 3.5 years. Here in this scripture passage in Micah 2 regarding End-Time Jacob, (God's covenant people), they are in their unfinished unrefined state. This is why the Holy Spirit refers to them here as **Jacob** and not Israel.

So here we come to an interesting question. Is this Bozrah Exile all just so much bad news? Or might it be "good grief"? Just what will be happening during the Tribulation period? And why might it be a good thing for the saints to fly off to this place of mystery out at the sheepfolds of Bozrah? Is it possible that the Bozrah exile will be more than just be an incarceration or exile story? Might the Bozrah enclosure also provide some degree of *shelter* and even *nurturing or spiritual nourishment* for the children of Abraham, Isaac, and Jacob in the end-time? Is Bozrah in fact a place of relative safety, "away from 666, away from the face of the dragon"?

Well as a matter of fact we do have some good solid evidence of this. The latter day exile of God's people will indeed be for their spiritual feeding and nurturing. Our other Scripture passage come from the book of Revelation chapter 12... And so to pick up the "rest of the story" our journey of inquiry takes us on into the New Testament and to the Apocalypse of the Apostle John. In the saga of 'the woman of Revelation 12' we see the story of an astounding massive exodus of people. Judging from Revelation 7 this company of Tribulation Saints probably numbers in the hundreds of millions. Here in this pivotal passage in Revelation 12 we see the flight of the woman, (a picture of God's covenant people), during the 666 period, the final 3.5 years of this age. She is given the wings of a great eagle. (What great country associated with the eagle might be involved here?) And her flight is "away from the face of the dragon". She flies off to "her place", her place of exile. And according to John's prophecy in Revelation 12:6 and repeated again in Rev. 12:14 the woman, (another handle on God's covenant people in the end-time), flies off to exile in Bozrah for two specific purposes.

1. She is there to be **protected**. And
2. She is there to be **fed, or nurtured**.

This Bozrah Exile must first and foremost involve a spiritual nurturing or nourishment. John sees this vision of the woman, (and in scripture this represents God's covenant people). She is given the wings of an eagle. And **on her own volition** she flies off to a place of nurturing for the said 1260 days or 3.5 Biblical (360 day) years. John's vision is clearly telling us a story of the end-time gathering Micah saw and his vision we see in Revelation 12 actually parallels the story of the gathering of Jacob in Micah 2:12-13. This gathering of Jacob involves the children of Abraham, Isaac, and Jacob, **and Joseph** in end-time. Bozrah is the place, (or places), where this exile takes place. This is where Jacob will be nurtured in the things of God for 1260 days - (Rev. 12:14), or 3.5 Biblical years - (Rev. 12:6). This is happening during the last half of the 70th week. This is precisely the time period of the Great Tribulation, the final 3.5 years of this age.

The Bozrah story apparently involves an end time gathering of God's single remnant Elect. During the Apocalypse the covenant people of God are being gathered from out of the Judeo-Christian people and the nations. This is all happening during the latter half of the 70th Week of Daniel. Jacob is wrestling with God once again, just as he did back in the times of the patriarchs.

THE BOZRAH DELIVERANCE AND THE YEAR OF JUBILEE.

The Bozrah story of the end-time is a dynamic yet untold story. It is a story of a climactic exodus and exodus even incarceration involving spiritual nurturing of all things, and finally a glorious deliverance at the end. Can any tome of mortal man top this story? Can any work of fiction even approach the splendor of this divine intervention at the close of this age? Is there anything that can approach the glory of this break-out by the returning Messiah in the Year of Jubilee?

The Bozrah story is yet to occur. It will be played out on earth before angels and men during the final 3.5 years of this age. See the article on 'The Woman of Revelation 12' This would be during the time of "Jacob's trouble". (Jer.30:7) Jeremiah clearly tells us that Jacob, God's covenant people, will get themselves into some serious trouble and tribulation by their compromises with the powers of this world. See this article. And yet he will be saved out of it.

The Bozrah deliverance, as we can see, is too awesome a story for our modern church and our present carnal Christian people to handle. Out of the crucible of Bozrah the silver (of redemption) and the gold of glory will be refined. God will refine His people "in the furnace of affliction/tribulation". (Isa.48:10) In the following verse He tells us why it must be this way. It is to bring God's people into a place of holiness where they will no longer pollute God's Holy Name.

Even Moses told the covenant people of God that this would happen to them. He said quite clearly that they would go into tribulation in the latter days.

DEUTERONOMY 4
29.....if from thence thou shalt seek the LORD thy God, thou shalt find him, if thou seek him with all thy heart and with all thy soul. 30 When thou art in **tribulation,** and all these things are come upon thee, even **in the latter days,** if thou turn to the Lord thy God, and shalt be obedient unto his voice; 31 (For the Lord thy God is a merciful God ;) He will not forsake thee, neither destroy thee, nor forget the covenant of thy fathers which he sware unto them."

The prophet Zechariah tells us the same story.
ZECHARIAH 13
13:9 And I will bring the third part through the fire,
and will refine them as silver is refined,
and will try them as gold is tried:
they shall call on my name,
and I will hear them:
I will say, It is my people:
and they shall say, The LORD is my God.

Our Apostle Paul fills in the story in Romans 11.
"And so all Israel will be saved". (Rom. 11:26)

O yes, all these wonders are yet to unfold into world history.

And they will, in the coming Day of Vengeance,
Even the long awaited awesome, climactic **Year of Jubilee**.

THE BOZRAH DELIVERANCE IN THE CONSTELLATION OF THE LESSER SHEEPFOLD OR "LITTLE DIPPER" AS SEEN BY THE PATRIARCHS

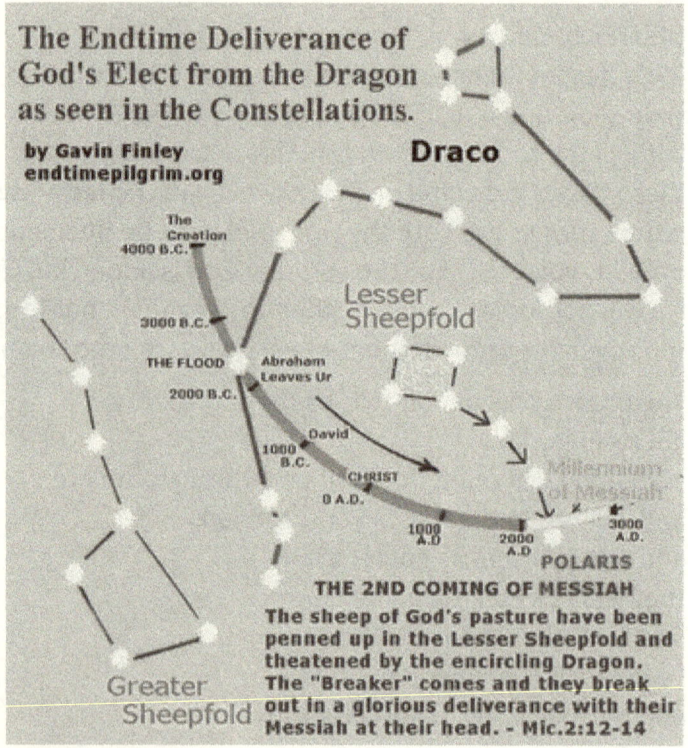

IN ANCIENT TIMES.

The very same story of a climactic deliverance and a breakout from a sheepfold is told in the constellations of the stars. The heavens are declaring the glory of God, and here His glory is in deliverance. The magnificent story is told in the constellation of the 'Lesser Sheepfold', Ursa Minor, or the 'Little Dipper'. Click on the image to the right to go to the article on the "Lesser Sheepfold" which outlines the connection of the Lesser Sheepfold to the story of the Bozrah deliverance.

Yes, the Bozrah story will be told eventually. Because it is an important spiritual place in which God will protect, preserve, refine, and nurture His people in the end-time drama. Apparently God thinks it is a big story as well. The heavens are telling this wonderful story. They are inscribed by God in the constellations of the stars.

Where will end-time Bozrah be located? Right now we do not know where Bozrah might be geographically. It may be many places. Or it may be one place. It may be one large central dumping ground for Judeo-Christian troublemakers and other 666 rejecters.

Oh yes, Bozrah is not just an ancient ruin. Nor is it just "past history". It is not just an archeological dig on a ruin of an ancient pastoral city of Esau southeast of the Dead Sea. For those who are there at this appointed place in the latter days this will be the place the prophets Isaiah and Micah spoke about. Bozrah will be a very real place under the control of modern day Edomites. It may well turn out to be a geo-political area far from the Promised Land. It may be a modern geo-political area out at the ends of the earth. The covenant people of God may look up in those days to find themselves in the place the Old Testament prophets spoke of over 2700 years ago.

And there, in that place they will find their God.
They will find Him

"...as rivers of water in a dry place,
as the shadow of a great Rock in a weary land." (Isa.32:2)

Find these articles and more by Gavin Finley MD at:
endtimepilgrim.org

Books written and edited by J. Scott Husted:

The Establishment: the fallen tent of David and God's end-time house of prayer

Beyond the Education Machine

Postcards From the Deeper Life – a spiritual classics reader

The Meat From the Mystics Series

These books and others are available at:
http://www.lulu.com/spotlight/scott_husted

www.ingramcontent.com/pod-product-compliance
Lightning Source LLC
Chambersburg PA
CBHW020803160426
43192CB00006B/424